# THE DOMESTIC ARCHITECTURE OF
# THE EARLY AMERICAN REPUBLIC
## THE GREEK REVIVAL

AT MAIN AND PLEASANT STREETS, NANTUCKET, MASSACHUSETTS
From a painting by Edward Stratton Holloway

# THE DOMESTIC ARCHITECTURE
## OF THE
# EARLY AMERICAN REPUBLIC
## THE GREEK REVIVAL

BY

HOWARD MAJOR, A.I.A.

WITH A FRONTISPIECE IN COLOUR AND
256 ILLUSTRATIONS

PHILADELPHIA & LONDON
J. B. LIPPINCOTT COMPANY
1926

*FIRST EDITION*

PRINTED BY J. B. LIPPINCOTT COMPANY
AT THE WASHINGTON SQUARE PRESS
PHILADELPHIA, U.S.A.

TO
**MY MOTHER**
AND TO
**MY WIFE**

# FOREWORD

NOT only the architect but the general reader should find the one style of architecture that America has developed to be of absorbing interest. Particularly is this true of the reader who is contemplating building himself a house : he and his architect will find this presentation of the best examples of this style throughout the country east of the Mississippi (our entire civilisation at that period) of the greatest practical value.

Architects, schools, colleges, architectural schools, libraries, and museums have long needed such an adequate body of illustrations of this style as has here been collected, and with it I have endeavoured to supply the story of this most interesting development—what it was, how it happened, its particulars, the adaptability of this style of domestic architecture to our use to-day, and its advantages.

To endeavour to cover the large field incorporated in the sway of the Greek Revival, a field ranging from the Gulf to the Great Lakes and from the Atlantic Seaboard to the Mississippi Valley, has involved the coöperation of many interested collaborators. I wish here to express my appreciation of their altruistic assistance and to acknowledge the value of their efforts in bringing this publication before the public—particularly to acknowledge the aid of two archeologists who have for years been devoting much time and careful thought to covering their respective territories in search of old edifices, men who

have been pioneers in gathering together works of the
Great Revival—Jefferson Hamilton, who kindly placed
his complete and well selected collection of photographs
of houses in Alabama, Florida, Louisiana, and Mississippi
at my disposal—Mr. I. T. Frary of the Cleveland Museum of Art for the fruits of his exhaustive researches
through Ohio, and to Mr. Edward Stratton Holloway,
of Messrs. Lippincott, for various suggestions.

And I further acknowledge my indebtedness to the
following :—

To Professor John S. Ankeney of the University of Missouri.
To Harry North Austin, for photographs about Natchez, Miss.
To Arthur T. Bolton, Curator of the Sir John Soane Museum,
 London, for chronological data upon the garden temple at
 Hagley.
To Mrs. J. F. Clark—Chairman, Division of Art, Ohio Fed-
 eration of Women's Clubs, for photographs in and about
 Columbus, Ohio.
To Ogden Codman for the use of his collection of architectural
 photographs.
To J. R. Coolidge, Jr. for several photographs of examples in
 Boston, Mass.
To N. C. Curtis, for helpful suggestions.
To Warren W. Day, for photographs in Illinois.
To Harold Donaldson Eberlein for his helpful suggestions.
To Robert Grannis for the excellent examples in Candor, Ithaca
 and Covert, N. Y.
To Paul Hollister for the interesting illustration from Grand
 Rapids, Mich.
To T. Charlton Hudson for the particularly interesting examples
 in Columbus, Ga.
To Fiske Kimball for the excellent photographs about Ann
 Arbor, Mich., and his kind coöperation.
To Robert A. Lancaster Jr., for his kind coöperation.

# FOREWORD

To A. J. MacDonald, Editor of *The Architectural Forum*, for his
assistance in many difficulties.

To William Odom for his interest and helpful advice.

To N. W. Overstreet for his help in Mississippi.

To Mrs. Marie B. Owen, Director, State Department of Archives
and History, Montgomery, Ala.

To Albert Simons for many of the photographs in Charleston, S. C.

To Douglass Taylor for procuring photographs in Huntsville, Ala.

To Howell Taylor for many photographs in Michigan.

To Reginald Townsend, Editor of *Country Life* for photographs in
Natchez, Miss.

To Alexander J. Wall, Librarian of the New York Historical
Society, for his aid in placing the photographic data of this
Society at my disposal.

To William T. Warren, for helpful data in Alabama.

To Russell Whitehead, Editor of the *White Pine Series* for his
great kindness in placing the valuable and comprehensive
photographic material of that publication at my disposal.

To Roger B. Whitman, Associate Editor of *Country Life* for his
interesting photograph in Northumberland County, Va.

To Frank P. Whiting, for his interesting photographs about
Cooperstown, N. Y.

To J. Appleton Wilson, Corresponding-Secretary, Maryland Historical Society, for the photographs in Baltimore, Md.

To Richardson Wright, Editor of *House and Garden*, for his kind
assistance in presenting photographs.

And to the following photographers:

R. T. Tebbs, for many excellent photographs through Georgia
and in Tusculoosa and in South Carolina.

Phillip B. Wallace, for the photographs chosen about Philadelphia.

John Wallace Gillies, for the photographs of houses in Great Neck,
Long Island.

Halliday Historical Photograph Company, for several photographs
in Massachusetts.

T. N. Henderson, for photographs in Natchez, Miss.

James F. Hughes and Company, for photographs in Baltimore, Md.

H. P. Tresslar, for the photographs in Montgomery, Ala.

# FOREWORD

## BIBLIOGRAPHICAL

Further, I acknowledge my indebtedness to Fiske Kimball's work, Domestic Architecture of the American Colonies and the Early Republic, for historical data and for the excellent analysis in its chapter on this period.

Other indebtedness to published work is hereby acknowledged to the following :

American Builder's Companion, The, by Asher Benjamin, 1816.

Architect or Practical House Carpenter, The, by Asher Benjamin, 1830.

Architecture of Colonial America, The, by Harold Donaldson Eberlein 1915.

Body of Architecture, The, by Isaac Ware, 1756.

Century of Missouri Art, A, by J. S. Ankeney, in the *Missouri Historical Review* of July, 1922.

Charles Bulfinch Architect and Citizen, by Charles A. Place, 1925.

Classical Antiquities of Athens, by Stuart and Revett, first volume appeared in 1762, second 1787, third 1794, fourth 1816.

Colonial Architecture of Maryland, Pennsylvania, and Virginia, The, by Joseph Everett Chandler, 1892.

Early Domestic Architecture of Ohio, by I. T. Frary, in the *American Architect* of April 11, 1923.

Encyclopedia Britannica, 11th edition.

English Ironwork of the XVII and XVIII Centuries, by J. Starkie Gardner, 1911.

Examples of the Greek Revival Period in Alabama, by J. Robie Kennedy, Jr., *The Brickbuilder*, for June, and July, 1904.

Furniture Masterpieces of Duncan Phyfe, by Charles Over Cornelius, 1922.

Georgian Period, The, edited by William Rotch Ware, 1899.

Greek Revival, The, by Howard Major, *The Architectural Forum*, February, 1924.

Greek Revival, The, Its Manifestation in England, by Howard Major, *The Architectural Forum*, March, 1924.

# FOREWORD

Late Georgian Houses, by Stanley C. Ramsay, 1919.

Modern Builder's Guide, by Minard Lafever, 1833.

Monumental Architecture in Great Britain and Ireland, by A. E. Richardson, 1914.

New Bedford of the Past, by Daniel Ricketson, 1903.

Octagon, The, by Glen Brown.

Old Northwest, The, by Fred Austin Ogg.

Old Houses of Michigan, The, by Fiske Kimball, in *The Architectural Record*, September, 1922.

Old Houses of Connecticut, by the Connecticut Society of the Colonial Dames of America, 1923.

Palladio.

Plans and Views in Perspective with Descriptions of Buildings, by Robert Mitchell, 1801.

Pioneers of the Old Southwest, by Constance Lindsay Skinner.

Ruins of Paestum, The, by Thomas Major, 1768.

Thomas Jefferson, Architect, by Fiske Kimball, 1916.

Vitruvius Britannicus, by Colin Campbell, 1715–71.

White Pine, The, edited by Russell F. Whitehead, 1916–26.

HOWARD MAJOR

New York and Palm Beach
June, 1926

# CONTENTS

CHAPTER                                                                         PAGE

I. Introduction . . . . . . . . . . . . . . . . . 3

II. An American Style for Americans . . . . . . . . 11

III. The Inception of the Style . . . . . . . . . . 17

IV. The Development of the Greek Revival . . . . . 27

V. Materials and Arrangement . . . . . . . . . . 53

VI. Variations and Structural Details . . . . . . . 59

VII. The Development West of the Alleghanies . . . . 83

Index . . . . . . . . . . . . . . . . . . 233

# ILLUSTRATIONS

PAGE

At Main and Pleasant Streets, Nantucket, Massachusetts
*Frontispiece*

The Gorgas House, Tuscaloosa, Alabama . . . . . *Title page*

Both from paintings by Edward Stratton Holloway

Sketch Plan for remodelling the Governor's House at Williamsburg,
Virginia, 1779, by Thomas Jefferson . . . . . . . . . 19

Maison Carrée, Nîmes, France . . . . . . . . . . . 21

Virginia State Capitol, Richmond, Virginia, 1789, designed by
Thomas Jefferson . . . . . . . . . . . . . . 22

Design for a Church in the Vitruvian Style, by Colin Campbell . 23

Garden Temple at Hagley for Lord Lyttelton, by James Stuart,
1758 . . . . . . . . . . . . . . . . . . . 29

No 15 St. James Square, London, by James Stuart, 1760 . . . 30

Design of a Greek Temple for Living Purposes, by Robert Mitchell,
1801 . . . . . . . . . . . . . . . . . . . 32

Thaddeus Burr House, Fairfield, Connecticut . . . . . . 35

Bank of the United States, designed by Benjamin Henry Latrobe,
finished by William Strickland . . . . . . . . . . 40

Professor's House, University of Virginia, Charlottesville, 1818,
designed by Thomas Jefferson . . . . . . . . . . 42

Arlington, Alexandria Co., Virginia . . . . . . . . . 46

Andalusia, near Philadelphia, 1835 . . . . . . . . . . 47

"Berry Hill", Virginia, 1835 . . . . . . . . . . . 48

Elevation from "The Modern Builder's Guide", 1833, by
Minard Lafever . . . . . . . . . . . . . . . 49

From "The Modern Builder's Guide", 1833, by Minard Lafever . 50

First Floor Plan of a Country Residence from Lafever's "The
Modern Builder's Guide", 1833 . . . . . . . . . . 54

Van Ness Mansion, Washington, D.C. . . . . . . . . . 54

House at Montgomery, Alabama . . . . . . . . . . 59

Design for a Country Villa from Lafever's "The Modern Builder's
Guide", 1833 . . . . . . . . . . . . . . . . 61

The Louis Hall House, Osborne, Michigan . . . . . . . 62

Triple Window, 1109 Walnut Street, Philadelphia . . . . . 63

Doorway of Mackay House, Willseyville, New York . . . . . 65

Doorway, 1107 Walnut Street, Philadelphia . . . . . . . 65

Portico Entrance, Andalusia, near Philadelphia . . . . . . 66

# ILLUSTRATIONS

PAGE

A Doorway at Portsmouth, N. H. . . . . . . . . . . . . 67
Doorway of Professor Seymour's House, Hudson, Ohio . . . . 67
Doorway, Treat House, Aurora, Ohio . . . . . . . . . . 68
Doorway of the Cox House, Dresden, Ohio . . . . . . . 69
A Doorway at Unionville, Ohio . . . . . . . . . . . . 69
Girard College, Philadelphia . . . . . . . . . . . . 71
Vesper Cliff, Oswego, N. Y. . . . . . . . . . . . . . 73
Interior of the John C. Stevens House, College Place and Murray
    Street, New York City . . . . . . . . . . . . . . 74
Cast Iron Balcony at Athens, Georgia . . . . . . . . . 76
Log Cabin at Logan Elm, Ohio . . . . . . . . . . . . 83
House at Tuskegee, Alabama . . . . . . . . . . . . . 89
"Gainswood", Demopolis, Alabama, built by General G. B. Whitfield 92
Singletary House, Streetsboro, Ohio, about 1835 . . . . . . 93
A Doorway at Claridon, Ohio . . . . . . . . . . . . 94

# PLATES

## THE NORTH ATLANTIC SEABOARD

PLATE

MAINE
    Ellsworth . . . . . . . . . . . . . . . . . . . 1
    Greely Residence, Ellsworth . . . . . . . . . . . . 2
    House on Danforth Street, Portland . . . . . . . . . 2
    House on State Street, Portland . . . . . . . . . . 3
    House on Spring Street, Portland . . . . . . . . . . 4
    Two-Family House, Portland . . . . . . . . . . . . 5
VERMONT
    Castleton . . . . . . . . . . . . . . . . . . . 6
MASSACHUSETTS
    House at Corner of Summer and Bedford Streets, Boston . . 7
    Henry Codman House, Roxbury . . . . . . . . . . 8
    Guild House, Roxbury . . . . . . . . . . . . . . 9
    Edward Everett Hale House, Roxbury . . . . . . . . 10
    Oak Knoll, Whittier House, Amesbury . . . . . . . . 10
    Booth House, Boston . . . . . . . . . . . . . . 11
    Roxbury . . . . . . . . . . . . . . . . . . . 12
    Doorway at 59 Mt. Vernon Street, Boston . . . . . . 13
    Old Bennett House, New Bedford . . . . . . . . . . 14
    Louisburg Square, Boston . . . . . . . . . . . . 15

# ILLUSTRATIONS

PLATE

CONNECTICUT

Home of Richardson Wright, Silver Mine . . . . . . . . . 16
New London . . . . . . . . . . . . . . . . . . 17
Sanford House, Litchfield . . . . . . . . . . . . . 17
Farmington . . . . . . . . . . . . . . . . . . 18
Thaddeus Burr House, Fairfield . . . . . . . . . . . 19
Doorways at New London . . . . . . . . . . . . . . 20

NEW YORK

The Boody House, Seneca Lake . . . . . . . . . . . 21
Hollenbeck House, Owego . . . . . . . . . . . . . 22
Daniels House, Owego . . . . . . . . . . . . . . 22
Marshall House, Rodsmans Neck . . . . . . . . . . . 23
Candor . . . . . . . . . . . . . . . . . . . 24
Ithaca . . . . . . . . . . . . . . . . . . . 25
Ithaca . . . . . . . . . . . . . . . . . . . 26
Staten Island . . . . . . . . . . . . . . . . . 27
Staten Island . . . . . . . . . . . . . . . . . 28
Staten Island . . . . . . . . . . . . . . . . . 28
Candor . . . . . . . . . . . . . . . . . . . 29
Front Street, Owego . . . . . . . . . . . . . . . 30
Cooperstown . . . . . . . . . . . . . . . . . 31
Preston House, Colliersville . . . . . . . . . . . . . 31
Willseyville, Tioga County . . . . . . . . . . . . . 32
Cooperstown . . . . . . . . . . . . . . . . . 33
Great Neck, Long Island . . . . . . . . . . . . . 34
Randolph . . . . . . . . . . . . . . . . . . 35
Great Neck, Long Island . . . . . . . . . . . . . 36
Miller House, Ludlowville . . . . . . . . . . . . . 36
Randolph . . . . . . . . . . . . . . . . . . 37
Montour Falls . . . . . . . . . . . . . . . . . 37
Harpersfield . . . . . . . . . . . . . . . . . 38
Harpersfield . . . . . . . . . . . . . . . . . 38
Doorway at Randolph . . . . . . . . . . . . . . 39
Doorway at Deruyter . . . . . . . . . . . . . . 39

PENNSYLVANIA

Andalusia, Bucks County . . . . . . . . . . . . . 40
John Price Wetherill House, Locust Grove . . . . . . . 41
The Flatlands, Audubon . . . . . . . . . . . . . 42
Roberts House, Walnut Street, Philadelphia . . . . . . . 43
Reed House, Chestnut Street, Philadelphia . . . . . . . 44
Portico Row, Spruce Street, Philadelphia . . . . . . . . 45

# ILLUSTRATIONS

PLATE

1109 Walnut Street, Philadelphia . . . . . . . . . . . 46
212 South 4th Street, Philadelphia . . . . . . . . . 47
Doorway, Mount Airy, Philadelphia . . . . . . . . . 48
Doorway 715 Spruce Street, Philadelphia . . . . . . . . 48

NEW JERSEY
Van Winkle Residence, New Market . . . . . . . . . 49
Houses at Metuchen . . . . . . . . . . . . . 50
Sebring Residence, Plainfield . . . . . . . . . . 51
Agnew Residence, New Brunswick . . . . . . . . . 52
Ewing House, Morristown . . . . . . . . . . . 53
Princeton . . . . . . . . . . . . . . . . 53
Doorway at Bordentown . . . . . . . . . . . . 54

DELAWARE AND MARYLAND
Wilmington . . . . . . . . . . . . . . . . 55
107 West Monument Street, Baltimore . . . . . . . . 56
119 West Franklin Street, Baltimore . . . . . . . . . 57
604 Cathedral Street, Baltimore . . . . . . . . . . 58
515 Park Avenue, Baltimore . . . . . . . . . . . 59
105 West Franklin Street, Baltimore . . . . . . . . . 60
118 West Franklin Street, Baltimore . . . . . . . . . 60
8 West Mount Vernon Street, Baltimore . . . . . . . . 61


THE OLD NORTHWEST
OHIO
Kelley House, Columbus . . . . . . . . . . . . 62
Norwalk . . . . . . . . . . . . . . . . . 63
Guthrie House, Zanesville . . . . . . . . . . . 64
Warren . . . . . . . . . . . . . . . . . 65
Talmadge . . . . . . . . . . . . . . . . 66
Phi Gamma Delta House, Granville . . . . . . . . . 67
Chagrin Falls . . . . . . . . . . . . . . . 68
House between Chagrin Falls and Solon . . . . . . . 69
House near Wellington . . . . . . . . . . . . 70
Hurst House, West of Rocky River . . . . . . . . . 71
Singletary House, Streetsboro . . . . . . . . . . 71
Baldwin Buss House, Hudson . . . . . . . . . . 72
House West of Ashtabula . . . . . . . . . . . 73
Norwalk . . . . . . . . . . . . . . . . . 74
Kirtland . . . . . . . . . . . . . . . . . 75
Pickering House, St. Clairsville . . . . . . . . . . 76
Gaylord House, Silver Lake . . . . . . . . . . . 76

# ILLUSTRATIONS

PLATE

East Porch, Kelley House, Columbus . . . . . . . . . 77
Doorway, Phi Gamma Delta House, Granville . . . . . . 77
Doorway of Baldwin Buss House, Hudson . . . . . . . . 78
Doorway, 405 Front Street, Marietta . . . . . . . . 78
Doorway, Elwell House, Willoughby . . . . . . . . . 79
Doorway at Madison . . . . . . . . . . . . . 79
Doorway, Buckingham House, Zanesville . . . . . . . . 80
Doorway, Western Reserve College, Hudson . . . . . . 80

ILLINOIS
The McKinney House, Peoria . . . . . . . . . . . 81
The Morron House, Peoria . . . . . . . . . . . . 82

MICHIGAN
The Pike House, Grand Rapids . . . . . . . . . . . 83
Smith House, Grass Lake . . . . . . . . . . . . 84
Ann Arbor . . . . . . . . . . . . . . . . 85
Mills House, Tipton . . . . . . . . . . . . . 86
James McAllister House, Tecumseh . . . . . . . . . 87
Tipton . . . . . . . . . . . . . . . . . 88
Smith Tavern, Clinton . . . . . . . . . . . . . 89
Colonel James R. Smith House, Monroe . . . . . . . . 90
David Carpenter House, Blissfield . . . . . . . . . 91
Anderson House, Tecumseh . . . . . . . . . . . . 92
Near Manchester . . . . . . . . . . . . . . 92
Thomas Howland House, near Adrian . . . . . . . . . 93
Butler Treat House, near Tecumseh . . . . . . . . . 93
Matthews House, near Clinton . . . . . . . . . . . 94
Dr. Mason House, Dundee . . . . . . . . . . . . 95
Peavey House, near Tipton . . . . . . . . . . . . 95
Doorway on La Plaisance Bay Road . . . . . . . . . 96

THE SOUTH ATLANTIC SEABOARD

VIRGINIA
Arlington, Alexandria County . . . . . . . . . . . 97
Mantua, Northumberland County . . . . . . . . . . 98
Berry Hill, Charlotte County . . . . . . . . . . . 99
The Archer Residence, Richmond . . . . . . . . . . 100

NORTH CAROLINA
Martichal Residence, Raleigh . . . . . . . . . . . 101
Doorway of the Martichal Residence, Raleigh . . . . . . 102

SOUTH CAROLINA
Mikell Residence, Charleston . . . . . . . . . . . 103

# ILLUSTRATIONS

PLATE

Mikell Residence, Charleston . . . . . . . . . . . 104
Rutledge and Montagu Streets, Charleston . . . . . . . 104
The Miller Residence, Charleston . . . . . . . . . 105
9 Bay Street, Charleston . . . . . . . . . . . . 106
Alston Residence, Charleston . . . . . . . . . . . 107
Ladson Residence, Charleston . . . . . . . . . . 108
Charles Alston House, Charleston . . . . . . . . . . 109
William Mason Smith House . . . . . . . . . . . 109
Charleston . . . . . . . . . . . . . . . . 110
Lanes Residence, Beaufort . . . . . . . . . . . . 111
Beaufort . . . . . . . . . . . . . . . . . 111

SOUTHEASTERN GEORGIA
Savannah . . . . . . . . . . . . . . . . . 112
An Entrance at Savannah . . . . . . . . . . . . 113
An Entrance at Savannah . . . . . . . . . . . . 113
A Cast Iron Balcony at Savannah . . . . . . . . . . 114
329 Abercorie Street, Savannah . . . . . . . . . . 114
Portico of Tellfair Art Gallery, Savannah . . . . . . . 115
Cast Iron Railing at Tellfair Museum, Savannah . . . . . 115
The Hermitage, Savannah . . . . . . . . . . . . 116

FLORIDA
Noaring House, Marianna . . . . . . . . . . . . 117
Ely House, Marianna . . . . . . . . . . . . . 117

## THE OLD SOUTHWEST

NORTHWESTERN GEORGIA
Columbus . . . . . . . . . . . . . . . . . 118
Columbus . . . . . . . . . . . . . . . . . 119
Fantaine House, Columbus . . . . . . . . . . . . 120
Columbus . . . . . . . . . . . . . . . . . 120
642 Prince Street, Athens . . . . . . . . . . . . 121
Athens . . . . . . . . . . . . . . . . . . 122
House on Prince Street, Athens . . . . . . . . . . 123
425 Hill Street, Athens . . . . . . . . . . . . . 124
Bradshaw House, Athens . . . . . . . . . . . . 125
La Grange . . . . . . . . . . . . . . . . . 126
Wilson House, La Grange . . . . . . . . . . . . 127
Dallis House, La Grange . . . . . . . . . . . . 127
W. Reeves House, La Grange . . . . . . . . . . . 128
Todd House, La Grange . . . . . . . . . . . . . 129
Hill House, La Grange . . . . . . . . . . . . . 130

# ILLUSTRATIONS

|  | PLATE |
|---|---|
| Numosa Hall, Roswell | 131 |
| Executive Mansion, Milledgeville | 132 |
| Emory Spear House, Macon | 133 |
| Coleman House, Macon | 134 |
| Ralph Small House, Macon | 135 |
| Dr. Miller's House, Macon | 136 |
| Atlanta | 137 |

ALABAMA

| Montgomery | 138 |
|---|---|
| Montgomery | 138 |
| D. L. Roseman House, Tuscaloosa | 139 |
| Cochrane Place, Tuscaloosa | 140 |
| Battle House, Tuscaloosa | 141 |
| Spence House, Tuscaloosa | 142 |
| President's House, University of Alabama, Tuscaloosa | 143 |
| Huntsville | 144 |
| Huntsville | 145 |
| Huntsville | 146 |
| Casey Homestead near Auburn | 147 |
| Rush Homestead near Tuskegee | 147 |
| Cobb House, Tuskegee | 148 |
| Tuskegee | 148 |
| A Cottage at Tuskegee | 149 |
| At Tuskegee | 149 |
| A Raised Cottage at Auburn | 150 |
| A Cottage at Auburn | 150 |
| Huntsville | 151 |

MISSISSIPPI

| Monmouth, Natchez | 152 |
|---|---|
| Stanton Hall, Natchez | 153 |
| Dunleith, Natchez | 154 |
| A Plantation Home at Natchez | 155 |
| Sargent House near Natchez | 155 |
| Auburn House, Natchez | 156 |
| A Plantation Home at Natchez | 156 |
| Rosalie, Natchez | 157 |
| Devereaux, Natchez | 157 |
| Natchez | 158 |
| General Grant's Headquarters, Vicksburg | 158 |
| Natchez | 159 |

# ILLUSTRATIONS

PLATE

LOUISIANA

232 Rampart Street, New Orleans . . . . . . . . . . 160

2221 Prytania Street, New Orleans . . . . . . . . . . 160

Baker Homestead, near Thibodoux . . . . . . . . . 161

A Plantation Home near Thibodoux . . . . . . . . . 161

Hermitage, Ascension Parish . . . . . . . . . . . 162

Three Oaks, near Chalmette . . . . . . . . . . . 162

Plantation House near Convent . . . . . . . . . . 163

Across River from New Orleans . . . . . . . . . . 163

Bayou St. John . . . . . . . . . . . . . . . 164

Stover House, New Orleans . . . . . . . . . . . 165

In the American Section, New Orleans . . . . . . . . 165

In Garden District, New Orleans . . . . . . . . . . 166

In Garden District, New Orleans . . . . . . . . . . 167

Beauregard Homestead, New Orleans . . . . . . . . 167

At Jackson and Chestnut Streets, New Orleans . . . . . 168

# CHAPTER I
## INTRODUCTION

# THE DOMESTIC ARCHITECTURE OF
# THE EARLY AMERICAN REPUBLIC

## THE GREEK REVIVAL

## I

## INTRODUCTION

THE best way to discover the need of a work of reference upon a given subject is to require such a reference and to learn that it does not exist. Heretofore our only important information regarding the Greek Revival has been contained in publications contemporaneous with the period. This notable and significant phase of American architecture has been neglected, with the exception of a chapter here and there and a few magazine articles, and at best these references have been widely scattered. It is the aim of this book to incorporate in as comprehensive a manner as possible all the various types of the domestic phase of this period in a volume companioning the vast amount of work published on the Georgian period in America, thereby complementing the subject of American architecture up to the year 1850.

In accomplishing this, two things are necessary. First, to bring to light the fallacy of the impression that the nineteenth century was devoid of artistic expression and is a period to be shunned, as any text book on the history of architecture will indicate ; secondly, to place before the public irrefutable evidence that this Greek Revival is America's national expression in architecture.

3

The general misapprehension, of this architecture is thus expressed by a well known author:

The classicism of the Classical Revival, on the other hand, was essentially and unalterably rigid in its adherence to the forms of antiquity and the archaeological manner of applying those forms. It was not an adaptation, it was, in very truth, a revival of the modes of two thousand years ago, a gigantic exhibition of architectural archaeology.

The weakness of the architecture of the Classic Revival was in its rigidity and inflexible resistance to efforts to adapt it to varied modern requirements.

Tiny temple-fronted houses were not domestic and were as unreal and architecturally unsatisfactory as stage settings viewed from the rear.

Such condemnation is usually ascribable to the lack of real familiarity with the work of the period; any amateur with a smattering of architectural knowledge will readily realise the unfairness of such criticism as he glances through the illustrations of this book.

Like most of the nomenclature of architectural styles the appellation "Greek Revival" is a partial misnomer as applied to American architecture. In truth it is a classic revival of the ancient architecture of Greece and Rome with a great predominance of Greek form, although the Roman expression beginning the movement persisted to some extent until the end. Many authors prefer the designation of Federal Architecture for this style, but although this is perhaps a more fitting title, it is only understood by the small minority. The spontaneous naming of this period the " Greek Revival " has taken hold and it is much to be doubted if any success will be attained by the endeavours of the idealists to alter this designation.

We have a clearly drawn historical factor to consider in the development of the Greek Revival. While the states of the Atlantic Seaboard had an established civilisation the western states along the Ohio and Mississippi Rivers were still in a pioneer, embryo stage as the style gathered its momentum. Naturally, then, the architectural expression of the comfortably established communities would differ widely from the hardy efforts of men struggling to establish themselves in a new country, men who had to adopt the means at hand to solve their architectural problems.

There were likewise also natural differences in the western development of the style in the South and in the North. From Virginia and the Carolinas many pioneers migrated west to the rich so-called "cotton belt" of the South in Alabama and Mississippi and with slave labour quickly found prosperity in this fertile land. Their first object was to build suitable homes and they endeavoured to outdo in splendour the fine mansions to which they were accustomed in the sections from which they migrated. With their prosperity, as means to an end, they were enabled to erect palatial mansions.

On the other hand, the pioneers of the Northwest area were of more humble circumstances and tastes. They migrated from New England, New York, and Pennsylvania, and were well equipped to face the hardships they were to meet in the new wilderness without slaves to do their bidding. These settlers were not of wealthy class and were obliged to resort to ingenious invention to house their families. In no period of American history is the contrast so sharp as between the palatial homes of this New South and the modest dwellings of the New North.

Furthermore, the strong influence of already existing architectural tradition affected the Greek Revival and instituted differences between the North and South along the Atlantic Seaboard. The colonial traditions of both sections carried through into the new style, although the North was now in a prosperous condition and its homes rivalled, if they did not surpass, those of the South in splendour and size.

Because of such marked geographical and stylistic boundaries and because of the comparatively short time during which the style flourished, it has been considered advisable to follow these four great subdivisions, including separately the work within each area, rather than to adopt a chronological order.

The groupings, then, as we have seen, comprise: First: the North Atlantic Seaboard, including all that region east of the Alleghanies and north of the Potomac.

Second: the South Atlantic Seaboard, including all that section east of the Alleghanies and south of the Potomac.

Third: the Old Northwest, including all that region west of the Alleghanies and bounded on the south by the Ohio River, on the west by the Mississippi River and on the north by the Great Lakes.

Fourth : the Old Southwest, including all that portion west of the Alleghanies and bounded by the Ohio on the north and the Mississippi on the west.

It is not the intention in this book to search through the old records of various communities to establish the absolute dates of the buildings illustrated : this period of approximately but thirty years, between 1820 and 1850, is too clearly defined to make this necessary. The dates which are given have been ascertained with as much accuracy as possible without this exhaustive research.

The real aim is to bring before the public all of the various domestic phases included in this period throughout the then settled America by means of photographic reproductions of the actual buildings. With the spreading of civilisation we must expect the demolition of older edifices to make way for those with more modern equipment. Within our time, many of these dignified Greek buildings have been torn down, so that this is a propitious moment in which to gather together all of the extant examples possible. An Historical Society * has secured one of these buildings for preservation, and other such purchases will doubtless follow. It is quite right that along the Eastern Seaboard the older Colonial edifices should take precedence in this respect, but it is high time that

---

*The Northern Indiana Historical Society has acquired for its home the old South Bend City Hall, a most interesting example of late Greek Revival.

Michigan, Ohio, Georgia, and Alabama should acquire for posterity some of these Greek Revival buildings, which are their only archaeological tradition. The Greek Revival is emerging from its days of calumny and neglect, and now, a hundred years after its ascendency, its appreciation is manifest. But a few years ago we knew of the wooden Greek temple under the sobriquet of " Carpenter's Classic " : to-day we look at it with new interest and recognise it as the architecture of the Early American Republic.

# CHAPTER II
## AN AMERICAN STYLE FOR AMERICANS

## AN AMERICAN STYLE FOR AMERICANS

THE Greek Revival is a style which readily adapts itself to present day use ; and it has unmistakable advantages. It is the only thoroughly American architecture. The traditional American belongs in a house of this national style, our independent creation in architecture. With its wide geographic field, from Florida to Maine, evidencing the skill of the early designers in adapting the style to highly varied climatic conditions, we have not only a national expression in architecture ; but one that is suited to the rigour of the Maine winters as well as to the tropical heat of Georgia and the Gulf States.

Florida is the present day frontier, the melting pot of the Union, the Cosmopolitan State. Instead of the travesty upon Latin architecture which prevails throughout its area, there should be a thoroughly American style to appropriately house its inhabitants. The houses of the Hellenic phase throughout the Gulf States, with their shaded, two storied verandas, often encircling the entire house, fulfil every requisite of climate, convenience, and *nationalism*. As it is true in the South, so it is in the North and West. Styles borrowed from Latin Europe and North Africa often fulfil climatic conditions ; but they can never express our *national* character.

It is a popular belief that the earlier, " Colonial,"

architecture is America's special contribution to the arts. This supposition, however, is now realised to be far from the fact. It is the once ridiculed Greek temple-home of the first part of the nineteenth century that is distinctly our independent gift to universal architectural development.

Many parallels to our Colonial designs are to be found throughout England, and the inquisitive may readily verify this statement by a comparison of the smaller English domestic work of the eighteenth century with contemporaneous American design. This similarity was first called to our attention in "The Georgian Period" published in 1901. It is now universally conceded by authorities in both countries, particularly by such recent writers as S. C. Ramsay in "Small Houses of the Georgian Period," London, 1919, and Fiske Kimball in "Domestic Architecture of the American Colonies," New York, 1922.

In the grip of the prevalent idea that Colonial architecture is our national style, one may well think startling the contrary view. The great mass of Colonial data earlier gathered and published supported this first belief; principally because there then existed for comparison few works illustrating and treating the smaller English houses corresponding in scale with our American domestic edifices. Though much architectural matter relating to the eighteenth century had been published in England, it invariably treated of large and elaborate edifices and so did not furnish evidence of the close parallelism existing between the Colonial residence and the Georgian house of corresponding scope in England. Nothing on so lordly a scale was attempted here as in our mother country, and the only comparison then generally possible was of the great English Manor house and our modest domicile. That the styles were dissimilar naturally became a quite obvious conclusion, however erroneous. But in the last few years evidence which is indeed amazing has been accumulating of the strong parallelism between the contemporaneous English Georgian and the American Colonial homes.

The similarity of such smaller English examples to our Colonial architecture was undoubtedly noted by some American architects visiting England, but was accounted for as being due to a reflex movement from America to England. Even Mr. Ramsay in his book as late as 1919 persists in this view. Mr. Fiske Kimball proves its fallacy in an indisputable manner in his " The Domestic Architecture of the American Colonies." His reasoning is well founded and the causes are now apparent. In outlying English shires and throughout the American Colonies the designing of the house fell either to the gentleman amateur or to the builder. Either schemed the home with the aid of English handbooks of which a great number were published and sold at reasonable prices. These books quickly found their way to America. Their popularity may be judged by the number of editions published, sometimes running to as many as ten or twelve printings. Whether, then, in outlying districts in old England or in the American Colonies, the same *motifs* found faithful copyists and naturally similar results were produced.

But this is not true of the Greek Revival. The employment of the classic temple for dwelling purposes and of the colossal colonnaded order predominating in Southwestern homes was independent of contemporaneous European influence. Here we have the individual expression in architecture of the American people, our own great national style, without parallel in the domestic architecture of Europe.

While much has formerly been written derogatory to this American style, much can and doubtless will be written in its praise. Invariably it has a monumental quality, and it is unsurpassed in its restraint. And yet into this monumental quality has been infused a certain *charm*—an elusive element to secure when it must be combined with such stately character, but undeniably attained.

" American domestic architecture made its independent contribution to universal development. Whatever may be thought, there can be no doubt that it endowed America with an architectural tradition, unsurpassed in the qualities of monumentality and dignity." This tribute of Fiske Kimball emphasises the solid truth that the great progress in law, liberty and the sciences in America during the first half of the century of our national existence was not unattended by an equally creative period in architecture.

# CHAPTER III
*THE INCEPTION OF THE STYLE*

# III

## THE INCEPTION OF THE STYLE

AFTER the separation from England, America naturally turned more to the Continent than heretofore and particularly to the ancient republics of Greece and Rome for inspiration in architecture as in government, and so became the inheritor of their free institutions and traditions and more eagerly assimilated the results of archaeological research.

The movement began with the adoption of Roman form introduced by the initiative of Thomas Jefferson. Just as Inigo Jones was the father of the Renaissance in England, so was Thomas Jefferson the father of the Classic Revival in America. Furthermore, Inigo Jones was the first great English architect, and likewise Thomas Jefferson was the first great American architect. History further repeats itself, for as after Jones other individuals became determining factors in English architecture, so after the initiative taken by Jefferson, others played similar rôles here.

Under Jefferson's leadership the South was first to feel this manifestation of direct classicism in the temple form of architecture. The first forms, derived from Roman antiquity, were subsequently almost entirely superseded by the Greek forms which were to predominate everywhere. Indeed so fully was Greek detail adopted later in the movement that the period became popularly known as the Greek Revival.

Jefferson imbued with the classic ideals and forms of the Romans, played such an important part in introducing this movement to America, that an account of the development of the style would not be complete without an outline of his architectural activities.

It is doubtful whether Jefferson gave serious thought to architecture until about 1769, when, at the age of twenty-six, he proposed building Monticello. Order and coördination were important factors in Jefferson's life. This, together with his legal training, equipped him with a sympathetic understanding of the teachings of Palladio with whose books he formed a life-long alliance.

In his earliest studies of Monticello we find little differing from the general architecture of the American Colonies, but, as these studies progressed, he gravitated toward Palladio and his final drawings show inspiration directly attributable to this source. Thus Jefferson was beginning to use classic Rome for inspiration, rather than to borrow from the architecture of the surrounding country.

His next architectural endeavour was in connection with the Virginia Commonwealth. About 1779, while Chief Executive of the State of Virginia, he made a sketch for the remodelling of the Governor's house at Williamsburg. In this he planned rows of eight columns across the entire front and rear, and specified a pediment-roof running from colonnade to colonnade. The result was an amphiprostyle, octastyle temple. Here, years before it would elsewhere reappear, Jefferson resurrected the temple of the ancients to be used for dwelling purposes. In it lies the distinctive characteristic of the Classic Revival that was to follow—a pediment carrying through and roofing the building without breaks. Previous to this sketch, this method of roofing had not been attempted. The pediment had heretofore been in-

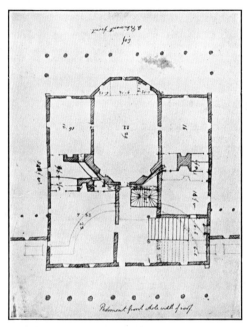

SKETCH PLAN FOR REMODELLING THE GOVERNOR'S
HOUSE AT WILLIAMSBURG, VIRGINIA, 1779
BY THOMAS JEFFERSON

dependent of the roof and abutted against it, the building being invariably wider than the portico.

It is not surprising that Jefferson should have employed this temple type. He was a man of individual thought and initiative, and as he was purposely turning away from the architecture about him and was a close student of Palladio's "Four Books of Architecture," in which were to

19

be found at that time the beſt reproductions of Roman temples, he naturally turned to this source. In the Governor's house, he had a square, box-like plan, obviously requiring a portico, and so his mind reverted to the Roman temples which he had admired in Palladio. Any of his contemporaries would have placed the four-column portico across the front, with the pediment independent of the main roof. Although this remodelling was abandoned, the temple idea was firmly rooted in Jefferson's academic mind and was further to expand when his European trip of 1784-89 gave him the opportunity of ſtudying the Antique at firſt hand.

Jefferson spent these European years travelling upon diplomatic matters, meanwhile acquainting himself with European architecture, of which he wrote and which he praised in his letters. On his southern trip, among the ancient monuments of Provence, he received the moſt enjoyment. He writes to the Countess de Tesse from Nîmes: "I am immersed in antiquities from morning to night. For me the city of Rome is actually exiſting in all the splendour of its empire." Here in Southern France he ſtudied the Maison Carrée, which was to become the prototype of the Virginia State Capitol. Upon the requeſt of the Directors of the Public Buildings in Virginia for him to consult an eminent architect for a plan for a State Capitol, he began, in 1785, sketches of a suitable building in the classic ſtyle of antiquity, using as a model the Maison Carrée. Then he consulted Clerisseau, the author of "Monuments de Nîmes," who made criticisms and suggestions which Jefferson incorporated with his own ideas. With modifications from the original, Jefferson produced this classic adoption of a Roman hexastyle temple, which was executed at Richmond, Virginia, in 1789. As in the sketches for the remodelling of the Governor's house, the portico

MAISON CARRÉE, NÎMES, FRANCE

bore a new relation to the building. Instead of being flanked by the body of the edifice, as in all cases heretofore, it alone constituted the entire *façade*.

Let us see the extent of Jefferson's contribution to architecture. His reproduction with variations of the Roman temple Maison Carrée is not quite the startling innovation that Mr. Fiske Kimball*contends. As a matter of fact, since the beginning of the eighteenth century many

---

*Domestic Architecture of the American Colonies and Early Republic, Fiske Kimball.

21

VIRGINIA STATE CAPITOL, RICHMOND, VIRGINIA, 1789
DESIGNED BY THOMAS JEFFERSON

22

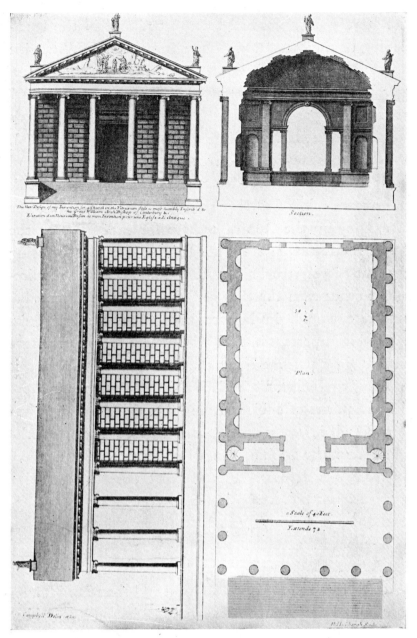

DESIGN FOR A CHURCH IN THE VITRUVIAN STYLE
BY COLIN CAMPBELL
Reproduced from Vol. II, Vitruvius Britannicus, 1731

23

small garden-temples had been reproduced in the land-scaping of English estates. In volume two of "Vitruvius Britannicus" Colin Campbell submitted a design for a "Prostile Hexastile Eustile" church, a design conceived between 1715 and 1731, sixty years previous to Jefferson's Virginia State Capitol building although never executed. This design is a reproduction of a Roman Ionic temple, and so far as the exterior is concerned is similar to Jefferson's endeavours. We find that many realised the *possibilities* of employing the Roman temple for modern use: the credit is due to Jefferson, not for the idea, but for being the first actually to build a temple for current require-ments other than the tiny garden house, which served as sculpture would, in landscaping. The Virginia State Capitol is important in that it is the first temple-structure erected for a purpose other than that of worship, and it is owing to Jefferson's initiative and desire to realise here the antiquities of ancient Rome that this movement was introduced into America. His Capitol preceded the Madeleine, the first important Roman temple of Europe, by twenty-two years. For the first time America led Europe in *actual erection* in a new architectural develop-ment, although the *idea* had also occurred to the minds of European architects.

Jefferson's importance as Secretary of State under Washington, and as Vice-President and then President of the United States gave him a powerful influence, which he exerted in advancing the interests of the Classic Revival in America.

# CHAPTER IV
## THE DEVELOPMENT OF THE GREEK REVIVAL

## IV

## THE DEVELOPMENT OF THE
## GREEK REVIVAL

WE HAVE seen that Jefferson introduced the Roman temple type into America. And the temple type prevailed. Later and in other hands probably ninety per cent of the temples erected were of the *Greek* orders while perhaps ten per cent were Roman, continuing even to the end of the period.

It is of the greatest interest to learn how this new American development became so overwhelmingly Greek that it is known by that name.

It is also necessary to see why the Greek Revival domestic architecture of America was an independent phase. The Greek Revival itself was universal to all European countries: the American domestic expression owes its independence to the fact that we adapted and built bona fide Greek temples for *homes* and developed many innovations. Europeans did not do this, although the *idea* was not foreign to them: as we shall see they even playfully designed, in a few instances, such houses, but evidently with no great expectation of ever building them. The description under the plate of such a building condemned it.

Although Jefferson introduced the Classic Revival into America and used his influence to promote it, another and even stronger factor was at work—the Classic Revival in Europe, particularly in England. The breaking away

27

from things English after the Revolution has been very much overdrawn. America continued to draw upon British architecture through the first years of the nineteenth century. In fact so intently did America continue to follow English leadership that as the Classic Revival became all prominent in England, so did it through this channel find its way to America.

In England the forces that led up to the classic revival began back in the days of Inigo Jones. The movement bore definite fruit in the early eighteenth century. The development was consistent with the constantly increasing data on classic ruins. In 1715 appeared the first English translation of Palladio by Giacomo Leoni, to be followed in 1729 by Colin Campbell's, and in 1735 with the version of Edward Hopper. The well known translation by Isaac Ware appeared in 1738. Many editions of these various interpretations of Palladio's work appeared, indicating the desire for knowledge of classic architecture. Thus was born the Roman Palladian phase which was to continue throughout the eighteenth century. Just after the middle of the century, many publications of the various ruins of ancient Rome appeared, thereby directing attention to the magnificence of Roman architecture. These publications quickly found their way into American libraries.

The birth of the *Greek Revival* in England dates back to 1762, when Stuart and Revett after exhaustive research in Greece published the first volume of their famous " Classical Antiquities of Athens " thereby enabling the curious to become familiar with Greek architecture.

The distinction of being the first architect of the Greek Revival of all countries belongs to James Stuart, the pioneer in Greek research. As early as 1758 he designed and built the previously mentioned Greek Doric

GARDEN TEMPLE AT HAGLEY FOR LORD LYTTELTON, BY JAMES STUART, 1758
The First Example of the Greek Revival in Europe

garden-temple at Hagley, for Lord Lyttelton, exhibiting his thorough knowledge of Hellenic architecture. This little garden-temple, although primarily erected to beautify the landscape, did have its utilitarian purpose, and it is but a short step to enlarge and partition the *cella* for dwelling purposes. This temple at Hagley, the first example of Greek Revival in Europe, is the prototype of the American Home of the following century. In 1760 Stuart gave origin to the Graeco-Roman school in his design for No. 15 St. James Square. Here Stuart exhibited his versatility by adapting Greek forms to the vernacular style of the Palladian school. The Graeco-Roman phase gathered in momentum in 1780 and endured until 1820. Of all the great English architects of

NO 15 ST. JAMES SQUARE, LONDON
BY JAMES STUART, 1760
The First Example of the Graeco-Roman School

the eighteenth century, there was not one whose influence was destined to be felt in the succeeding century as was Stuart's. However, he had limited opportunities, as, being in advance of the popular trend, his commissions were few. At this time the style of the " Brothers Adam " justly controlled the field, not only in England, but also in

30

America, far eclipsing Stuart and his contemporaries. Yet his pioneer labours instantly acted as a check to the Palladian school and somewhat aided the Adam's manner of classical restraint.

Of this Graeco-Roman school S. P. Cockerell (1754–1827) was particularly interesting, because of his pupil Benjamin Latrobe, who came to America to practise in the beginning of the century.

Of the architecture of the Graeco-Roman phase none, excepting an isolated example here and there such as the Greek garden-temple at Hagley, indicated an understanding of the spirit of Greek architecture. However, much Hellenic knowledge was being circulated and absorbed. Public opinion was slowly accepting Greek refinement and dignity. The exponents of the Greek phase were now devoting their whole attention to the transplantation of Hellenic art to England and by 1820 the movement had gathered its full momentum.

In the meantime we even find the transition from the *garden-temple* to the *temple-home*. In 1801 Robert Mitchell published " Plans and Views in Perspective with Descriptions of Buildings." On plate sixteen is illustrated a Greek temple with the *cella* of two stories divided for living purposes. But his own comments upon this temple-home were highly instructive as reflecting the English attitude throughout their Greek Revival upon this scheme of dwelling :

Whilst the three last plates which are inserted in this work are intended to elucidate the three styles of architecture (Greek,

31

Roman, and Gothic) they are offered at the same time as designs for mansions, or residences of persons of distinction, for which it is conceived, they are particularly appropriate, as the form of the temple admits of the highest magnificence. The better to render this applicable, if such designs should be thought worthy to be adopted, the plan, Plate 15, is annexed, in which it will be found that convenience has not been sacrificed to external appearance. If the designs, Plates 16 and 17, had been intended only to elucidate the subject of the styles of the Grecian and Roman architecture,

DESIGN OF A GREEK TEMPLE FOR LIVING PURPOSES, BY ROBERT MITCHELL, 1801

there would have been a propriety in confining the subject to the usual plan of the simple parallelogram or oblong square, with the peristyle, but as these designs were likewise intended for mansion houses, a deviation from this form has been adopted more suited to that purpose, for a design confined to the simple plan of the *Greek temple would be found as inapplicable to a modern mansion, as the Greek tragedy has been experienced to be unfit for the English stage.*

*Logically,* Mitchell was quite correct; but the fact remains that the American provincial half-baked methods happened to develop it into a lovely style.

Here is found, some fifteen years prior to its American appearance, the adoption of the Greek temple for the requirements of the family. These English publications within a few months found their way to America, where no such feeling as the temple being inapplicable to dwellings existed. It only awaited the enthusiast to carry the scheme into execution, which when once attempted spread like wildfire throughout the entire United States. There can be no doubt that Mitchell's publication played a most important rôle in America's adoption of the temple dwelling.

The fact is that the use of the *Greek* temple for domestic purposes did occur to English architects, but they felt that it would be inapplicable to this employment and the English public abided by their judgment so that any Greek temple dwellings, existing in England are merely *divagations* from the generally current modes. In America, on the contrary, the idea was embraced to its fullest extent: the Greek Revival became the practically universal style of architecture, and was *adapted by Americans to all the varied American conditions*—extremes of climate, extremes of character, temperament, social life and means; to every kind of environment and employing many local materials. It is an independent American development in architecture.

The British version of classicism was a combination of Roman planning and Greek orders and a not unhappy *ensemble* was its result.

Very soon after the publication in England of works

upon Greek antiquities, we find records of them having found their way to America. In 1762 copies of Thomas Major's " Ruins of Paestum " had been acquired by the Library Company of Philadelphia. In 1770 copies of Stuart's " Antiquities of Athens " were also to be found in the stock of the same company. America now embodied the Greek *orders* as presented by English publications, but did not follow their interpretation of current Hellenic *structures*. The very antagonistic spirit towards British dominance which sprang up in the first decade of the nineteenth century put an end to our conforming to the English architectural tradition which had thrived since the earliest colonial days.

But as in England, our craftsmen were delighted to avail themselves of the innovation of using these new forms in lieu of the overworked Roman orders. In 1790 we find the first authentic example of the Greek order used in the Thaddeus Burr House at Fairfield, Connecticut. From then on this order was to be adopted with a growing popularity.

Up to near the end of the eighteenth century the craftsman or gentleman amateur was alone responsible for the architectural design. From then the professional architect began to appear in America. The first, receiving their education in Europe, migrated to America. James Hoban who attended the architectural school of the Dublin Society arrived in South Carolina in 1789 where he erected the State House at Charleston. Later he built the President's House at Washington. Stephen

THADDEUS BURR HOUSE, FAIRFIELD, CONNECTICUT
The First Authentic Example of the Greek order in America

35

Hallet arrived from France in the same year. Benjamin Latrobe, of whom I have already written, crossed in 1796 and exerted a tremendous influence. His design for the Pennsylvania Bank had a profound effect throughout the country. Latrobe, after severing his relations with Cockerell, did a considerable amount of domestic work in England before sailing for America. His position was unique as an exponent of architectural ideals and tendencies current in both England and America. He was, in fact, one of the strongest, if not indeed the strongest, architectural link between the Old World and the New in his day and generation. He derived his inspiration from, and matured it in, England; and then further developed his style in his American practice. George Hadfield, one of the first to study in Rome, was well prepared to design his well known portico at Arlington, Va. As time went on Americans took up the practice and joined their ranks.

Robert Mills and Strickland, both pupils of Latrobe, also exerted strong influence upon the development of the style. Mills did many superb things, most of which, unfortunately, have disappeared. His design for the Pennsylvania State Capitol at Harrisburg was a masterpiece, and it is much to be regretted that it was never built. William Strickland, too, did admirable work, both civil and domestic, especially in Philadelphia.

During this time there also appeared highly educated men in affluent circumstances, men who had travelled in Europe and who could devote much of their time to the study and practice of architecture. Their training was derived from travel, observation and bibliographical research. Their architectural masterpieces speak for the efficiency of their early self-training. This fact together with their amount of work places them in the professional ranks.

Of this class we have Jefferson, L'Enfant, Thornton and Bullfinch. Of Jefferson we have heard. Major Pierre Charles L'Enfant, the cultivated French engineer arrived from France the end of the eighteenth century. He won recognition by his excellent plan for Washington, D. C. Doctor William Thornton was born in the West Indies in 1761 and educated in London. He travelled extensively while in Europe. He arrived in Washington in 1793 where he designed the first Capitol Building. He exerted an important influence upon the architectural field. Charles Bullfinch was born in Boston August 8, 1763 and died in 1844. In June 1785 he embarked on a pleasure tour of Europe where he took a keen interest in the architecture of England, France and Italy.

He returned in January 1787, and as he was in affluent circumstances, became a dilettante at architecture, first helping friends with the planning of their homes, then gradually taking up the work as a self-trained professional.

Although his life extended practically throughout the Classic Revival period, we have no data on his professional career after 1830, when his services on the National Capitol Building were completed.

The period of his life from 1818 to 1830 was almost exclusively devoted to the execution of Thornton's plan for the Capitol. Therefore it is not surprising to find very little trace of the Greek Revival in Bullfinch's work.

In 1828 Bullfinch designed the Maine State House in the then prevailing Greek style.

There are also to be considered the talented craftsmen of these days; craftsmen with a natural aptitude, who developed their architectural judgment to such a degree that they were enabled to successfully compete with the professional element and so deserve a ranking in that class.

Amongst these men were McComb, McIntyre and Benjamin. John McComb, born in 1763, ranks first of the New York men in his time and day. His work includes that architectural gem, the City Hall of New York, and St. John's Church. Samuel McIntyre, a carpenter, builder, and a wood carver of ability, designed many of the excellent buildings in Salem, Massachusetts, in the late eighteenth century and in the first quarter of the nineteenth. Asher Benjamin, of Greenfield, another carpenter architect, designed buildings in that vicinity. Later he moved to Boston, practicing throughout Massachusetts. He was better known by his popular architectural handbooks of which many editions of each publication were printed.

Of less importance were Alexander Parris in New England, Thomas Carstairs and Thomas Walter in Philadelphia. Other architects, although otherwise unimportant, are of particular interest because they designed domestic buildings in purely Greek manner. They include Elias Carter in New England, Ithiel Towne, M. E. Thompson, A. J. Davis, George Harvey, J. C. Brady and Minard Lafever of New York.

Lafever indicates the enthusiasm of two of the afore mentioned for the Greek manner in his preface of " The Modern Builder's Guide " 1833. This work is exclusively devoted to Greek Revival architecture. " I have also consulted several able and experienced architects in the vicinity, especially Mr. J. C. Brady (now deceased), and Mr. Martin E. Thompson, of this city. The plan of this work was sometime since submitted to the inspection of these two gentlemen, and they were pleased to say, that it met with their entire and cordial approbation."

From now on, with the temple style introduced by Jefferson in the Virginia State Capitol and with the Greek Doric order introduced in the Burr house, the growth and development of the style was to be persistent. In 1799-1801 Latrobe designed and built the Bank of Pennsylvania in the temple form, with Greek Ionic orders. In 1819 to 1826 the Bank of the United States was built by Latrobe upon the lines of the Parthenon. It is of vital interest that the Virginia State Capitol preceded the Madeleine in Paris, the first of the great European reproductions, by twenty-two years and that the Bank of the United States antedated the foreign version of the Parthenon, the National Monument at Edinburgh, and the Walhalla at Regensburg by ten years.

The few architects of this time were interested in

BANK OF THE UNITED STATES, DESIGNED BY BENJAMIN HENRY LATROBE, FINISHED BY WILLIAM STRICKLAND

public buildings and it was neither deemed necessary nor customary to employ professional advice for domestic work, and furthermore, in outlying districts the architect did not exist. Consequently the home was left to the devices of the interested amateur and craftsman, and from books and previously erected edifices they copied the order.

It is indeed interesting to learn how these two previous statements are confirmed by an author of nearly one hundred years ago. "I consider it necessary that all practical *house carpenters* should be fully acquainted with the orders of architecture, particularly those who reside in the *country*, where they have *no opportunity* of *consulting an* architect."* The temple form for public buildings was before them. In 1817 Jefferson had built Pavilion VII for the University of Virginia, a professor's house with a classroom to be sure, but primarily for domestic purposes, a Roman Doric temple supported on an arcade. The germ of the temple home was thus planted, and together with Mitchell's temple house, in his publication of 1801, the idea was fixed in the minds of the amateur designers. Furthermore, with little study of the Greek orders and their simple, bold mouldings, these novices could design an architectonic dwelling. Their ingenuity with the simple requirements then customary enabled them to fit rooms within the confines of the *cella*, with the consequent result that in the twenties these small Greek dwellings were springing up everywhere.

---

* "The Architect or Practical House Carpenter," 1830, by Asher Benjamin.

The architect refrained from such a simple expedient as not allowing sufficient scope to his imagination. In fact it was fortunate for the Hellenic domestic architecture of America that there were few architects. In the hands of amateurs, precisely because of their lack of

PROFESSOR'S HOUSE, UNIVERSITY OF VIRGINIA, CHARLOTTESVILLE, 1818
DESIGNED BY THOMAS JEFFERSON

knowledge, the style developed individuality and created America's independent expression of the Greek Revival.

On the contrary, by this time in Europe the architect was a well established factor and left but few and unimportant dwellings in the hands of the amateur. Therefore, then, European architects determined the national expression and *like the American architect* avoided

42

the cut and dried limitations of the temple plan, as exemplified in Mitchell's contemporaneous criticism " for a design confined to the simple plan of the Greek temple would be found inapplicable to a modern mansion, as the Greek tragedy has been experienced to be unfit for the English stage."

In America a radical change in sentiment was gathering momentum during the first decade of the nineteenth century. Up to this time we had been relying upon the mother country to form our opinions in literature and art. The causes which soon led to the War of 1812 were rapidly freeing us from this state of mind. Furthermore the French Revolution, with the resulting disorganisation, brought us a particularly large influx of cultivated Frenchmen. The conditions in France were such that the *emigrés* came almost wholly from the educated classes. Naturally the influence of French civilisation, intensified by the memory of that country's aid in our dark hour, would have a marked influence upon America. The architecture of the French Empire was marked by an austerity of design and solidity of form based upon architectural formulas which America was now ready to assimilate.

It is interesting to note the French influence in the dress of the time as related by Mrs. Frances Trollope upon her visit to New York in 1829. She remarks that French fashions absolutely prevailed, and that in walking down Broadway she could scarcely believe that she was not in a French town, as she noted the costumes of the men and women. It is not surprising then to discover French influence in the decorative arts, particularly in the fields of furniture and decoration. The architecture was synchronous and correspondent with this sway of the Empire styles in furniture. Although the Classic Revival is often accredited to the strong anti-English sentiment after the American Revolution, it is rather a matter of evolution, as the English styles persisted for forty years and England had by this time adopted the Greek Revival.

But the War of 1812 together with the sympathy for things French marked the complete severance from English domination of American thought. In all the arts America from now on was to be independent, at least independent of England.

In the first quarter of the nineteenth century there arose a coterie of literary lights who attained international recognition, of which Washington Irving was the leader. With James Fenimore Cooper, William Cullen Bryant, and others they were creating a distinctly American literature, as were the amateur architects evolving a distinctly American architecture. Expressing the spirit of the times, James Kirke Paulding was ranting in his writings against any English dominance in political as well as literary and artistic affairs.

The War of Greek Independence, 1821–1827, gave the final impetus to the Hellenic movement. America with outstretched arms embraced things Greek in every phase of life. Strongly in sympathy with this cause, there developed throughout the country a "Greek" mania. A gentleman from western New York declared he could furnish, from his sparsely settled region, " five hundred men six feet high, with sinewy arms and case-hardened constitutions, bold spirits and daring adventurers, who would travel upon a bushel of corn and a gallon of whiskey per man from the extreme part of the world to Constantinople "—and within a hundred years such sentiment is annihilated by the Eighteenth Amendment. Our country, it seems, is one of varied moods and extreme views, often swayed by sentimentality. To such lengths did we go, in the past as now, that then we gave our towns Greek appellations. To realise the universal extent of Greek enthusiasm at this period it is but necessary to review a few of the names adopted throughout then civilised America. For instance, examples may be cited in various sections; first in the North Atlantic States, Alesia and Timonium in Maryland ; Euclid, Parnassus, and Ulysses in Pennsylvania ; Alpha, Athenia, and Sparta in New Jersey; Corinth and Troy in Vermont ; Milo, Troy, and Athens in Maine ; Athens, Sparta, Delphi, and Corinth in New York. On the Southern Seaboard, Sardinia, Eureka, Troy, and Omega in South Carolina; Athens, Ypsilanti, Sparta, and Ionia in Georgia; Palmyra, Ionia, and Phoebus in Virginia ; Aurora and Palmyra in North Carolina. In Florida, not annexed to the Union until 1821, such towns as Athens, Eureka, and New Troy appear. In the old Northwest, Ypsilanti, Ionia, and Scio in Michigan ; Bucyrus, Xenia, Adelphi, and Omega in Ohio ; Attica, Delphi, and Scipio, in

45

Indiana; Carthage, Troy, Eureka, and Metropolis in Illinois; Sparta, Troy, Palmyra, and Ixonia in Wisconsin; Carthage, Palmyra, and Athens in Missouri. In the old Southwest, Olympia, Corinth, Eureka, Athens, and Plato in Kentucky; Athens, Delphia, and Sparta in Alabama;

ARLINGTON, ALEXANDRIA CO., VIRGINIA

Corinth, Delta, Eureka, and Acme in Mississippi; Sparta, Delta, Homer, and Atlanta in Louisiana. Nothing could better illustrate the prevalence of Greek thought throughout the states and territories of the Union than the way in which names of towns were borrowed from Greece.

At this time, 1826, George Hatfield added to Arlington, Virginia, the Doric temple portico, after the temple of Paestum, a composition of six great Greek Doric columns ably terminating the commanding vista across the Potomac from Washington.

Nicholas Biddle in remodelling his country house

46

at Andalusia, near Philadelphia in 1835, achieved the extreme innovation of surrounding his dwelling with a colonnade, thus forming a periſtyle temple inſtead of the more frequent proſtyle arrangement.   It is intereſting to

ANDALUSIA, NEAR PHILADELPHIA, 1835
The Home of Nicholas Biddle

note that Biddle, a layman, had been the firſt known American to travel to Greece, in 1806.   In England nine out of ten architeꞓts completed their ſtudies by a visit to this land of classic architeꞓture, but America, the devotee of the Hellenic phase, found none of its architeꞓts able to take this opportunity.   Therefore, it is not surprising that Biddle should be the first to render this radical interpretation. All that was now essential for the fullfilment of Greek ideas was a transplanting of the Parthenon itself for domestic usage. This was realised in 1835 at "Berry Hill," Virginia, with eight columns in front instead of the usual four or six.

During the War of Greek Independence, myriads of Greek houses sprang up all over the country. The orders and details were carefully reproduced from imported restorations of the Greek orders and from American hand-

"BERRY HILL," VIRGINIA, 1835

books, such as Asher Benjamin's later editions and Minard Lafever's "The Modern Builder's Guide," published in 1833. It is interesting to note the conservatism of Asher Benjamin in his publications. In his 1816 edition none of the Greek orders are illustrated. In his editions as late as 1856 the Greek orders and detail are amply illustrated, but not an example of a Greek Revival house is shown and he proclaims: "Since my last publication, the Roman School of Architecture has been entirely changed for the Grecian." "The Architect, or Practical House Carpenter," 1830.

Lafever now takes the foreground in American pub-

FRONT ELEVATION FOR A COUNTRY RESIDENCE

ELEVATION FROM "THE MODERN BUILDER'S GUIDE", 1833, BY MINARD LAFEVER

49

lications and illustrates plans, sections, and elevations of the typical Greek home of the day and in his successive editions illustrates additional houses. Lafever and the later Benjamin editions disregard Colonial detail and devote their plates to Greek detail, including that of doors, windows, cornices, trims, etc. A quotation from

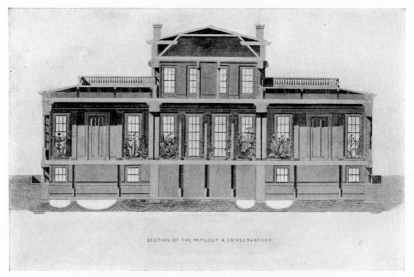

SECTION OF THE PARLOUR & CONSERVATORY

FROM "THE MODERN BUILDER'S GUIDE", 1833, BY MINARD LAFEVER

Lafever expresses the independence of the American mind towards British architecture: " From the work of Mr. Nicholson of London I have received a greater amount of aid than from any other source. (This was a treatise on geometry and construction and not on architecture.) The only other authors to whom I owe acknowledgement are Messrs. Stuart and Revett of London, from whose highly valuable and popular work, entitled 'The Antiquities of Athens,' I have borrowed the article relating to the 'Ancient Orders of Architecture.' "

# CHAPTER V
## MATERIALS AND ARRANGEMENT

# V

## MATERIALS AND ARRANGEMENT

BRICK and wood as building material continued in use from the preceding Colonial period ; the frame building, as previously, greatly predominating. The wood siding was frequently used on the principal façade with boards laid with flush joints instead of clapboards. Shingles for sidewall coverings were completely discarded. The usual pilaster at the corner successfully butted the clapboards, and if the pilaster did not exist, corner boards were introduced, as the clapboards were not mitred at the corners. After 1800 a great vogue for stucco began and continued throughout the period. It was often ruled to imitate ashlar or marble. Brick lost in favour and when employed was painted a light grey to effect stucco. Cut stone, practically unused before 1800, became a not uncommon material in the large cities of the Northern Seaboard and in the country communities adjacent to stone quarries. Occasionally marble was employed. Cast iron for the first time came into general usage and became one of the prominent materials of the period. Elaborate Corinthian capitals, columns, trellises, railings, window grilles, and other ornaments cast in iron became common features and were probably the most delightful artistic expression of the nineteenth century.

In plan the flexibility of arrangement seen in the houses preceding the temple type had to be subordinated to classical symmetry. The entire mass now being the

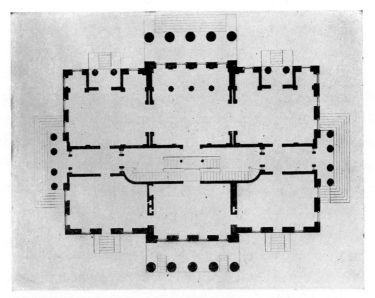

FIRST FLOOR PLAN OF A COUNTRY RESIDENCE FROM LAFEVER'S "THE MODERN
BUILDER'S GUIDE", 1833

VAN NESS MANSION, WASHINGTON, D.C.

54

firſt and greateſt consideration, convenience and intereſting planning were necessarily sacrificed although many
ingenious arrangements were evolved with the aid of
the supplementary side-wings, as seen in the plans from
Minard Lafever's "Modern Builder's Guide." In its
simpleſt form, the small four-column temple-dwelling,
the removal to one side of the ideal centre doorway was
required so as to allow for a room across the remaining
two bays. In the Van Ness House, Washington, 1813–
1819, a one-ſtory four-column portico was brought out
from the entrance doorway, of sufficient depth for a
carriage to drive under. This *porte cochère* was to become
an indispensable feature of any home of any pretensions
in the laſt half of the century.

# CHAPTER VI
## VARIATIONS AND STRUCTURAL DETAILS

## VARIATIONS AND STRUCTURAL DETAILS

MANY modifications of the Greek temple appeared
everywhere, particularly weſt of the Alleghanies.
But the moſt diſtinctive variation was in the Southweſt,
where a cubical house preceded by a row of columns

HOUSE AT MONTGOMERY, ALABAMA

was without a pediment or roof, as in the accompanying
illuſtration of a house at Montgomery, Alabama. It was
in this form of the Greek Revival that the connois-
seur firſt recognised the merits of the ſtyle, and these old
Southern plantation houses won favourable recognition
years ago. The Southweſt was never carried away with
the " temple home " type, but contented itself with the
colossal Greek colonnade and Greek detail. Undoubtedly

59

this mode was due to the influence of the preceding period, when the desire to screen a flat roof from view was paramount. It is not strange then that these Greek Revival Southern homes should usually be known to the uninitiated as " Southern Colonial." *

Occasionally an odd number of columns composed the portico, as in the Van Vorst mansion in Jersey City, now demolished. Another deviation in the North was the addition to the temple proper of two well subordinated wings at right angles to the axis of the main building, as shown in Lafever's plate here reproduced. It is in this form that many interesting variations occurred, and the *chef d'oeuvre* of the North are to be found. Much greater flexibility in planning and a graceful piling up of the composition to the central mass were attained in this solution of their problem. In the largest residences the scheme was carried a step further, with the transverse wings terminating with subordinated pavilions with colonnades and pediments parallel to the main body, producing a well-balanced and monumental three-part composition.

Frequently but one transverse wing was added, indicating the freedom of the designer from the shackles of the style; but the result was unbalanced, showed an unfinished composition, and was not satisfactory.

---

*Many of those Classic Revival houses are illustrated in one of the first comprehensive works on Colonial Architecture, "The Georgian Period. A collection of papers dealing with 'Colonial' or XVIII Century Architecture in the United States" 1899, although they belong to this later Period of 1820 to 1850.

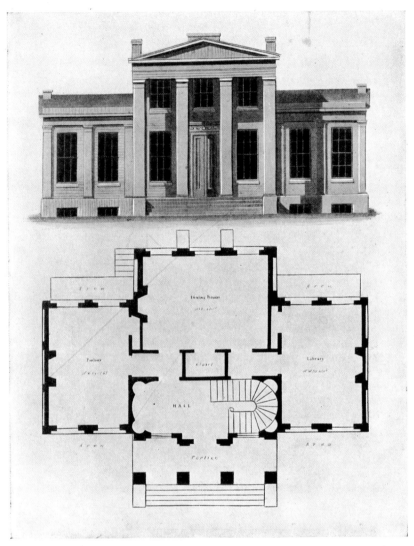

DESIGN FOR A COUNTRY VILLA FROM LAFEVER'S "THE MODERN BUILDER'S GUIDE", 1833

61

The temple ſtripped to its simpleſt form, that of the *cella*, appeared without the portico. The flat gable was retained on its narrow end, which was towards the ſtreet. The full Greek entablature was carried around the entire house. Often this type had one or both low transverse wings similar to the appurtenances of the

THE LOUIS HALL HOUSE, OSBORNE, MICHIGAN

colonnade-temple described above. It is to be recalled that a long, narrow Colonial house would have its broad side toward the ſtreet, in contradiction to the narrow front of the Greek house.

Another amusing and not uninteresſting interpretation of the temple-body with subsidiary side-wings was evolved, as in the Louis Hall House. The wings were each roofed with a half-pediment butting againſt the central wing, so that if the central wing were taken

away and the wings pushed together, a perfect pedi-
mented building would be formed.

The circular-head window, popular at the beginning
of the century, was practically abandoned, but the flat-
headed triple window which came into vogue in 1810

TRIPLE WINDOW, 1109 WALNUT STREET
PHILADELPHIA

frequently appears. It was of pleasing composition and
proportion; an excellent example was 1109 Walnut Street,
Philadelphia, now demolished. The casement window
running to the floor of the portico often occurs, used sometimes with casement sash and sometimes with triple sliding
sash. Another innovation is the "frieze" window in the
entablature just under the eaves. As we shall see, the full
Greek entablature encircled the building, and the wide

63

frieze suggested the possibility of windows of the depth of this frieze. This expedient was quickly adopted to light and ventilate the otherwise useless attic space. To make this small, shallow window seem a part of, and decoration of, the frieze, either a cast iron or carved wood grille was fitted flush with the face of the frieze.

The narrow window frame in brick walls with a four inch brick reveal was retained after its adoption in the first years of the century. The sash-bar was reduced to its minimum width, producing very delicate divisions of the sash.

The brick opening of the windows was perfectly plain with flat arches, although stone lintels, often moulded and decorated, were prevalent. As the period progressed, the stone lintel became more common, assuming heavy proportions and with overdecorated detail as the style declined. In some instances the brick courses were carried through over the window-head without arch or lintel. Often the window of the main story had a stone architrave of a simple band, not moulded, with elaborate lintel, generally supported by consoles.

The usual form of doorway included sidelights with a squared transom, although it was not exceptional to find elliptical or circular transoms or no transom at all. Other variations are many, from the simple door enframed with architrave to the door crowned with squared, elliptical, or circular transoms, as the doorway at 1107 Walnut Street, Philadelphia. Doorways were frequently framed with square *antae* with intermediate columns on axis with the mullions of the side lights, as in that of the

DOORWAY OF MACKAY HOUSE, WILLSEYVILLE, NEW YORK

DOORWAY, 1107 WALNUT STREET, PHILADELPHIA

65

Mackay House. Often the square *antae* framed the simpler doorway without the intermediate columns. Then too they were framed with fluted and reeded architraves with corner blocks and centre blocks in place of the key, as in the accompanying illustration of a doorway at

PORTICO ENTRANCE, ANDALUSIA, NEAR PHILADELPHIA

Portsmouth, N. H. In the simple, unadorned doorways, as that of Professor Seymour's house at Hudson, Ohio, engaged or freestanding columns flanked the entrance, with an entablature, generally without the pediment. When, however, four columns flanked the doorway, the pediment was more often employed, as in the portico entrance to Andalusia. In the Northwest, further variations are noted as in the doorway at Unionville, Ohio, in which a remarkable use is made of consoles the height of

66

A DOORWAY AT PORTSMOUTH, N. H.

DOORWAY OF PROFESSOR SEYMOUR'S HOUSE, HUDSON, OHIO

the transom, supported by the columns, and terminating in square corner-blocks. In the Cox House at Dresden, Ohio, the panelled lintel rests on the ftone *vosoirs* which enframe the otherwise plain jamb. Another amusing

DOORWAY, TREAT HOUSE, AURORA, OHIO

innovation is found in the Treat House at Aurora, Ohio, in which an elliptical transom has bands of ftars interspersed with reeding in lieu of the usual fan light.

In a few of the more pretentious houses the Greek columns were of heavy, ancient proportions, but in the majority of cases they were somewhat attenuated. This practise was advocated by Asher Benjamin in his publication of 1830, particularly when applied to private

DOORWAY OF THE COX HOUSE, DRESDEN, OHIO

A DOORWAY AT UNIONVILLE, OHIO

69

houses. " I confess myself to be an admirer of Grecian architecture, yet I am not disposed to condemn the general proportions of the Roman orders, none of which, except the Doric, differ essentially from those of the Grecian. The column of that order was generally made, by the Greeks, about five diameters in height; but the same order, by the Romans, from seven and a half to eight diameters in height. It is, therefore, evident that the latter proportions come nearer to our practice than the former one, especially when the orders are used in private houses. The members of the Grecian columns and entablatures, however, are certainly better proportioned to each other than those of the Roman."* Often square piers or *antae* are employed in lieu of the column, as they were much less expensive to produce. As we have seen, the Greek Doric order was the first introduced, and it continued in favour for many years. About 1830 the Greek Ionic gained precedence, and in the middle thirties the Corinthian of the Lysicrates type came into vogue, following the striking example on the exterior of Girard College, 1833–47.

The almost invariable characteristic of the Hellenic phase was the complete surrounding of the building with the full entablature, in contradiction to merely carrying the cornice around, as in Colonial work. This characteristic will almost invariably determine this period even if none other is apparent. The mouldings were bold and heavy in strict accordance with the Greek profile. To quote Asher Benjamin, "these latter (Grecian mouldings)

*"The Architect or Practical House Carpenter," 1830, Asher Benjamin.

GIRARD COLLEGE, PHILADELPHIA

Thomas W. Walter Architect

An early example of the "Monument of Lysicrates type" of capital which created favour for this order during the last years of the style

71

are composed of parts of ellipses, parabolas, hyperbolas and other Ionic sections, and consist, mostly, of *large, bold* parts, which are so strongly marked, that each member of the profile is plainly seen at a very considerable distance."* The cupola, adopted in the eighteenth century, continued in use. Well designed ones were a common feature, and are to be found throughout the entire territory of the period, particularly in the large houses of the old Southwest and of the North Atlantic Seaboard, as at Vesper Cliff, Oswego, N. Y.

The interiors were marked by simple wall-surfaces with attention concentrated upon structural members and functional necessities, such as doorways, windows, fireplaces and the centre-pieces of ceilings. Panelling was not included in the scheme of decoration. Even the dado was omitted in favour of big, broad surfaces. As in the exterior, the full entablature was carried around the room. The rooms were not isolated, but opened into each other, partially screened by pilasters, columns, and entablature. The effect of stateliness was produced at the expense of intimacy. The interiors were bold and dignified, composed of straight, severe lines with heavy detail. The walls were severely plain plastered surfaces. The rooms were high studded with a carefully arranged disposition of windows, doorways, and chimney-piece. The doorways were wide, and together with the column partition the principal rooms of the first floor opened into each other with extensive vistas, but with a consequent lack of

---

*"The Architect, or Practical House Carpenter," 1830, Asher Benjamin.

privacy. The interiors displayed not a little ſtateliness and grace and lent themselves to large gatherings with the decorous formality which went hand in hand with cultivated taſtes and the rigorous thought of the time.

VESPER CLIFF, OSWEGO, N. Y.

The chimney-pieces were often of black marble with plain Doric pilaſters or engaged columns without the over-mantel of Colonial days. Door and window archi-traves were fluted, reeded, or a combination of both, with full contour of ingenious silhouette, symmetrical upon a central axis. It was successfully terminated at the

73

INTERIOR OF THE JOHN C. STEVENS HOUSE, COLLEGE PLACE AND MURRAY STREET, NEW YORK CITY

Alexander Jackson Davis Architect

From the original drawing in the New York Historical Society, by the courtesy of the Society

corners by inserting square blocks, which were turned or carved in bold relief. Sometimes the head-trim was of different section than that of the jamb-trim, by which means interesting variety was introduced. Frequently a long middle block in lieu of a key was substituted, this being carved in relief. Strangely enough this trim was far from Greek in derivation, but it was one of the products of the style and harmonised perfectly in its setting. It long outlived the Greek Revival and continued well throughout the last half of the century, to its ultimate detriment and subsequent unpopularity. The wide range of method and varied silhouette of this form of enframing an opening will ensure its rebirth in the not distant future.

As previously mentioned undoubtedly the outstanding decorative feature of the style was its ornamental cast iron, which heretofore had been used only in rare instances but was to continue in popularity long after the period had drawn to a close.

The casting of molten iron into ornamental shapes was done in Sussex, England, as early as the fourteenth century. It gained no vogue, however, and was rarely utilised. During the eighteenth century, cast iron, because of its character, found usage in the vase-shaped finials surmounting the standards of the wrought-iron railings.

Isaac Ware in his " Body of Architecture " 1756, page 89, remarks:

Cast iron is very serviceable to the builder and a vast expense is saved in many cases by using it; in rails and balusters it makes

CAST IRON BALCONY AT ATHENS, GEORGIA

76

a rich and massy appearance when it has cost very little, and when wrought iron, much less substantial, would cost a vast sum. But, on the other hand, there is a neatness and finished look in a wrought iron that will never be seen in cast, and it bears accident vastly better.

The first architectural work wholly of cast iron was the seven great gates for St. Paul's churchyard in London, in the first quarter of the eighteenth century. It was not, however, until one hundred and ten years later, with the advent of the Classic Revival, that cast iron came into great popular favour, to the practical exclusion of the wrought metal. The appearance of the steam engine, 1760–1770, and of the railroad, in 1825, gave to the iron-foundry industry a great impetus, and the process of manufacture was brought to perfection in 1860.

During this period ingenious ornamental casting appeared throughout the country. In contrast to the refined and attenuated wrought shapes of the preceding period there was seen Greek rendering of classic *motifs*, robust designs in splendid scale with the monumental character of the architecture. The cast-iron work in the first sixty years of the nineteenth century is not only the most artistic expression of the century, but an expression that will stand comparison in the entire field of American decorative arts. In the sixties the design degenerated rapidly into realistic expression and inappropriate usage.

With the extensive growth of scientific investigation in the second quarter of the nineteenth century, the preponderant interests of the cultivated public and of its creative minds swung away from artistic creation to that of scientific development. The great industrial revolution of the nineteenth century diverted to itself most of the creative energy which for many years past had found expression in artistic form. Robert Fulton and Samuel F. B. Morse are such examples of the spirit of the century: men who began their careers as painters, and who left examples of their work which bespeak of their skill in an art which was later crowded out of their lives to make way for their better known scientific contributions.

As this scientific and industrial movement gained its full momentum about 1850, and creative minds were turned in its direction, the arts waned and the Greek Revival drew to a close, to be followed by a second "Moyen Age." It is interesting to learn the disrepute into which a quarter of a century later the period had fallen, a disrepute itself due to the almost universal bad taste into which the country unhappily had lapsed. Daniel Ricketson in 1873 wrote as follows: "The house (Joseph Rotch house about 1823) was much injured in appearance by its heavy Tuscan (undoubtedly Greek Doric) columns of wood, a fashion improperly adopted from the temple architecture of the ancient Greeks and Romans, but now abandoned in private buildings, for which we are indebted in a great measure to the judicious criticism of the late Andrew J. Downing." Again he writes, "Our court house (New Bedford) was built about the year 1830 at the time when the pseudo-Greek style of architecture was in vogue. It is a substantial structure of brick and internally well arranged and comfortable, but the heavy Tuscan (Greek Doric) columns of wood disfigure it greatly." Thus continued the condemning criticism which, begun in 1842 by Andrew Jackson Downing, has remained in vogue until recently. In 1848 Mrs. L. G. Tuthil spoke of the " Greek Mania " as having passed. However, one may well wonder how much the Greek Revival has to do with the present Classic Revival which began in the nineties. Certainly there are today many strivings similar to those of one hundred years ago.

# CHAPTER VII
## THE DEVELOPMENT WEST OF THE ALLEGHANIES

# THE DEVELOPMENT WEST OF THE ALLEGHANIES

THE close of the American Revolution found the United States in ownership, by the treaty of peace with England, of a vaſt tract extending weſtward from the Alleghanies to the Mississippi, and northward to Canada and the Great Lakes. The section lying north

**LOG CABIN AT LOGAN ELM, OHIO**
Authentic and typical log cabin of the early western settlers moved from a near–by farm to its present location

of the Ohio River, the Northweſt of the young Republic, is now popularly known as " The Old Northweſt." The tract from the Ohio River south to the Gulf is similarly known as " The Old Southweſt."

Prior to the war, settlers had begun invading these Indian lands weſt of the Alleghanies. Within a few years after the successful termination of hoſtilities, immigration began at an extensive rate and the movement of " Weſtward Ho! " had begun. However, the danger of Indian uprisings was ever present, and these frontiersmen were forced to devote as much time to arms as to the plough. The frontier home was a primitive affair of log walls and rarely of larger size than single length logs would permit. On an average they were from twelve to fourteen feet wide and from fifteen to eighteen feet long. Sometimes these cabins were divided into two rooms, with an attic above, but frequently there was but one room. The logs were halved together at the corners, and the space between filled with moss or clay or covered with bark. In the earliest times the roof was of bark ; later on shingles were used.

It was not until the close of the War of 1812–1815 that the country was freed from Indian disturbances and the settlers were enabled to devote themselves exclusively to their own advancement and profit. With peace a swift revival of immigration again swept over the country and upon a heretofore unprecedented scale. By about 1820 many of the settlers had acquired sufficient means to consider suitable homes, also many in this second wave of *migration* came prepared to build, not cabins, but houses. The West was now ready to develop an architecture.

It was at this time, when *migration* to the West was in full swing, that the Greek Revival had gained its great momentum along the seaboard. The parallel goes further—the *first* beginnings of the Greek Revival had been contemporaneous with the *first* extensive immigration into the new territory. We can conclude that the development of the West and the Greek Revival were born simultaneously, and together reached maturity.

As the West ceased to be a frontier development, the rude log cabins and stockaded trading-posts gave place to architecturally studied houses and villages, and it was natural, too, that the trading, professional, and land-owning classes, following close upon the heels of the first hardy trappers and settlers, should introduce the architectural characteristics of the sections from which they came.

America was not only creating an individual architecture, but she was creating different expressions in each of the four great sub-divisions. At no time in the architectural development of the nation was there such a distinct line of demarcation as between the Greek Revival of the old Northwest and the old Southwest upon a line marked by the Ohio River.

The streams of migration into the Northwest flowed from many sources. New England contributed heavily to Marietta, Cincinnati, and many rising river-towns on the Ohio. That part of Ohio on Lake Erie drew largely from Connecticut. Many Pennsylvanians migrated west through their state to eastern Ohio. Virginians and Carolinians came through Kentucky to southern Ohio and Indiana. Thus the Northwest territory became a melting pot of the Colonies. The settlers from the Virginias and the Carolinas and Kentucky were of little education or were even illiterate. Indeed, many of them had sought the West to escape a society in which the distinction of birth had put them at a disadvantage. The settlers from New England were as a rule people of some education.

The Southwest, accessible from the Southern Seaboard, was settled by immigration from Maryland, the Virginias, and the Carolinas, with a French influence along the lower Mississippi from the old province of Louisiana.

There was a time when the frontier folk of the trans-Alleghany country from the Lakes to the Gulf were much alike — all pioneer farmers and stock-raisers absorbed in the conquest of the wilderness. But by 1820 the situation had altered. Under the play of climate and industrial forces, the West had divided into a North and South. Climate, soil, the cotton gin, and slavery combined to make of the Southwest a great cotton-raising area of large plantations, interested in the same things and swayed by the same impulses as the Southern Seaboard. Wealthy, educated planters with great retinues of slaves were migrating to this rich cotton-belt from the southern tidewater states. Their manners, customs, and institutions were transplanted beyond the mountains. There was the same political rivalry between the slave-holding planters of the " Blue Grass " and the " poor whites " of the mountain districts that there was in Virginia between the tidewater planters and the mountaineers. On the contrary, economic conditions made the Northwest a land of small farms, free labour, town-building, and diversified manufactures and trade.

The Southerners of Kentucky and Tennessee migrating north of the Ohio were of the poorer whites, the more democratic non-slave-holding Southern element. The New Englanders who migrated were mainly those having difficulties in making ends meet; poor, discontented, restless, without influence, and needing only the incentive of cheap lands in the West to sever the slender ties which bound them to the East.

Even amongst the first of the Southern pioneers there is reference to slaves being brought into the Southwest, which fact was soon to effect the prosperity of this territory and to create the cleavage between the North and South. This cleavage began with the opening of the nineteenth century. The slave enabled the planter in the cotton-belt to operate extensive plantations and quickly to attain wealth undreamed of by the Northern pioneers. This wealth in turn allowed the Southern gentlemen to build homes of suitable importance. On the other hand the Northerners, lacking slaves and the rich agricultural soil of the South, their prosperity was slow and limited, which reflected in their homes, which were of a most modest character. Everyone is familiar with the large so called " Colonial " houses of the old Southwest, but very few indeed are acquainted with the contemporaneous houses of the old Northwest : this is because of the palatial character of the Southern house as compared to the modest character of the Northern one. Even the *Georgian Period* includes within its scope of Colonial architecture much of this Southwestern work of the Greek Revival. An idea of the palatial character of a typical residence of the time may be gleaned from a quotation from the *Brickbuilder* of 1904: "'The Cochrane Place,' what a scene of hospitality this name must bring to the mind of the old inhabitant, who perchance was a guest there in the old days. It was built by Dr. William Cochrane in 1840. The shafts of the Corinthian columns were brick and the fluting *in situ*, the large capitals being of cast iron. Each column is said to have cost the owner six hundred dollars. The door knobs and escutcheons were until recently of sterling silver." Nothing upon such a scale was even thought of in the Northwest, but the Southwest was filled with such palatial homes. The Southerner almost invariably adopted the style of the Classic Revival, unlike the Northwest where Colonial buildings were being erected hand in hand with those of the Classic Revival. The Southerner resorted to a predetermined plan and exterior composition of two stories with the colossal colonnade. The hall ran through the house with rooms on either side and its kitchen and service in outbuildings—an idea borrowed from the Southern colonies. The composition was a box-like mass with a row of six or eight columns across the front, without the usual pediment found throughout the East, as shown in the accompanying illustration of the house at Tuskegee, Alabama. With this almost universal composition it is remarkable that these buildings should show such rich variety. It would seem, with an accepted plan and two-story composition of portico, that one plantation house would bear close

resemblance to any other, but on the contrary there was a
great variety in expression. Although the " Greek Mania " was manifeſt in the Southweſt it only affected their
architecture to the extent of including Greek orders and
detail with the Roman. The temple form of home was
studiously avoided. The Southweſt, in its architectural

HOUSE AT TUSKEGEE, ALABAMA

expression, ſtood aloof from the reſt of the country. In
this Greek Revival phase they contributed another
national expression in architecture. America's national
expression in the temple home may be criticised as " out
of character," but the national architecture evolved in
the Southweſt was admirably " in character " with its setting and semi-tropical climate. With such appropriate
tradition, it seems poor taſte for Florida to succumb to the
grotesque imitations of Spanish architecture so totally at
variance with our Anglo-Saxon temperament. We might

89

better "carry on" our inheritance of this semi-tropical American type of architecture.

The Southerner took many liberties with the order. The height of the entablature was often reduced and the columns attenuated. It was not uncommon to omit the architrave in carrying the entablature around the building. This feature was unlike the earlier method of merely carrying the cornice through and differed from the full entablature carried around elsewhere. Porches and balconies for each floor, as in the houses of eighteenth century Charleston, were very desirable for the climate of the South. The Southerner of the nineteenth century often carried on this Charleston tradition by inserting second story balconies between or just behind the columns, the full width of the colonnade, allowing the "Colossal" order to run the height of the building. If this was not done a small balcony almost invariably projected over the centre doorway. These well shaded second floor balconies furnished a cool retreat during their tropical summers.

The side walls were without pilasters or other decoration and were neglected to allow their luxuriant vegetation to screen them, both from the eye and from the rays of the sun. Often, however, a colonnade completely encircled the building. To further insure cool interiors, very high studded walls prevailed. The first floor was located from one to five feet above the ground level. The larger houses in the country were all of two stories.

An interesting exception to the general arrangement

is Gainswood at Demopolis, Alabama, built by General G. B. Whitfield. The composition, a main body with subsidiary wings and porches, was carefully studied, and the result is successful and interesting from all four sides. The plan also deviated from the accepted type by employing a mezzanine floor. Undoubtedly we can account for this departure as due to the efforts of one of a party of educated Frenchmen, exiled from the Court of Napoleon, who sought refuge on our shores. The Federal government granted them a large tract of land in Demopolis on condition that the vines and olives should be cultivated.

Alike in both the Northwest and Southwest, outside of a very few important buildings, the houses were built without architects, the owner or builder himself acting as the designer; and the homes they evolved portray their character. The rare instance of an architect being employed in an outlying district is found in the President's house at the University of Alabama at Tusculoosa. This was due to the fact that the house was one of the units of a monumental scheme. Mr. Nichols, an Englishman then of Philadelphia, was brought to Tusculoosa by the State to do the State Capitol and the University buildings. The professional touch is evident in the basement story, an unusual feature of the period, which supports the colossal Ionic order.

In the Northwest since economic limitations were great, utilitarian considerations were of first importance. Ingenuity was not stifled by lack of affluence, and we

"GAINSWOOD" DEMOPOLIS, ALABAMA, BUILT BY GENERAL G. B. WHITFIELD

find widely variegated types of plan and elevation in homes suitable to small farms and villages because of the invention displayed by those of fragile means. It is in this greater freedom and variety of design that the Northwest varies from the other three territories embracing the Greek Revival.

The Southern whites in the Northwest were of

SINGLETARY HOUSE, STREETSBORO, OHIO. ABOUT 1835
Illustrating the continuance of the Colonial phase in the Northwest after its end in the East

the illiterate class, while emigrants from the North were generally educated. It is not surprising then to find the Northern settler determining the architecture, while the Southerner played no part in this development.

The early settlers in this territory had left the East before the Greek Revival had gained precedence and for the most part they were totally unfamiliar with it, being only conversant with the preceding Colonial styles of the seaboard. Furthermore they were acquainted with, and could easily acquire architectural handbooks of the day, handbooks that were now quickly losing their earlier popularity in the East. They, therefore, built Colonial homes, as the Singletary house at Streetsboro, Ohio, and the doorway of the house at Claridon, Ohio, that savour

A DOORWAY AT CLARIDON, OHIO
Illustrating the Colonial Adam phase of the West persisting after
its end in the East

Strongly of New England and the northern seaboard States. They were even building these houses after 1820 when the style was practically dead in the East, and continued this practice until the middle of the century. It was an Indian Summer of Colonial architecture. Probably it persisted as late as it did in the West because of a natural desire of the settlers to surround themselves with an environment reminiscent of the towns and villages from which they came.

The arrivals of the second wave of emigration, after the War of 1812–1815, were familiar with the Greek Revival which had taken such a strong hold along the seaboard, and it was they who were to carry and introduce this Hellenic movement to the Northwest. In building they selected the now fashionable style of the East, and this style quickly found root and began to flourish. The hardy settler because of difficult and expensive transportation must needs resort to means and materials at hand. The Greek orders and details were followed, but the expression was free and the *motifs* varied. The temple-type of dwelling was not the universal expression as it was in the Northern Seaboard. As far as possible materials on the site or in the community were employed, and a great variety of them were used in the building.

This lack of transportation at the beginning of the century was the greatest handicap to building. The government, realizing the necessity of a highway to the West for promoting national unity and strength, conceived a route starting at Cumberland, Maryland, passing through the Alleghanies to Wheeling on the Ohio River, and hence across the state. By 1818 it was opened to Wheeling; Columbus was reached in 1833, and Indianapolis about 1840. This artery, known as the National Road, has long since lost its importance; but then it was the connecting link between the East and the West and

95

up to 1860 was teeming with traffic. In 1825 the Erie canal had been opened and these two routes of travel at last made it easy for materials from the East to reach the homebuilders of the West. It is, therefore, along these arteries and the rivers and lakes that we find many of the examples of the Hellenic architecture of the Northwest.

In summing up the general characteristics of each territory are as follows:

*In the Northern Seaboard* the temple type with or without subsidiary wings predominated almost to the exclusion of any other type.

*In the Southern Seaboard* the temple and late Southern Colonial form swathed in Greek or Roman detail went hand in hand, both being equally popular.

*In the Old Southwest* cubical, box-like structures, often without roofs, preceded by a colossal colonnade or completely surrounded by colonnades predominated almost to the exclusion of other forms. The great number of large manor houses with high studded rooms was in direct contrast to the more modest dwellings of the old Northwest.

*The Old Northwest* is distinguished by its great variety of types, Greek buildings contemporaneous with Colonial. The Greek phase was marked by great variations with no marked type predominating. The necessity of colonnaded fronts was not felt and the general scale of the houses was most modest. These characteristics of the Northwest were a natural outgrowth of social conditions and a heterogeneous population.

PLATES

# THE NORTH ATLANTIC SEABOARD

*MAINE, VERMONT, MASSACHUSETTS, CON-*
*NECTICUT, NEW YORK, PENNSYLVANIA,*
*NEW JERSEY, DELAWARE, MARYLAND*

MAINE

PLATE 1

ELLSWORTH, MAINE

PLATE 2

GREELY RESIDENCE, ELLSWORTH, MAINE

HOUSE ON DANFORTH STREET, PORTLAND, MAINE

PLATE 3

HOUSE ON STATE STREET, PORTLAND, MAINE

PLATE 4

HOUSE ON SPRING STREET, PORTLAND, MAINE

PLATE 5

TWO FAMILY HOUSE, PORTLAND, MAINE

*VERMONT*

PLATE 6

CASTLETON, VERMONT

MASSACHUSETTS

PLATE 7

HOUSE AT CORNER OF SUMMER AND BEDFORD STREETS, BOSTON
Now destroyed

PLATE 8

HENRY CODMAN HOUSE, ROXBURY, MASSACHUSETTS

PLATE 9

GUILD HOUSE, ROXBURY, MASSACHUSETTS

PLATE 10

EDWARD EVERETT HALE HOUSE, ROXBURY, MASSACHUSETTS

OAK KNOLL, WHITTIER HOUSE, AMESBURY, MASSACHUSETTS

PLATE 11

BOOTH HOUSE, BOSTON

PLATE 12

ROXBURY, MASSACHUSETTS

PLATE 13

DOORWAY AT 59 MT. VERNON STREET, BOSTON

PLATE 14

COUNTY STREET FRONT OF OLD BENNETT HOUSE, NEW BEDFORD, MASSACHUSETTS
Built by John Avery Parker in 1834

PLATE 15

LOUISBURG SQUARE, BOSTON

CONNECTICUT

PLATE 16

HOME OF RICHARDSON WRIGHT, SILVER MINE, CONNECTICUT. 1840

PLATE 17

NEW LONDON, CONNECTICUT

SANFORD HOUSE, LITCHFIELD, CONNECTICUT

PLATE 18

FARMINGTON, CONNECTICUT

PLATE 19

THADDEUS BURR HOUSE, FAIRFIELD, CONNECTICUT, 1790

PLATE 20

DOORWAYS AT NEW LONDON, CONNECTICUT

NEW YORK

PLATE 21

THE BOODY HOUSE, ROSE HILL, SENECA LAKE, NEW YORK, 1838

PLATE 22

HOLLENBECK HOUSE, FRONT STREET, OWEGO, NEW YORK

DANIELS HOUSE, MAIN STREET, OWEGO, NEW YORK

PLATE 23

MARSHALL HOUSE, RODSMANS NECK, NEW YORK

PLATE 24

CANDOR, NEW YORK

PLATE 25

ITHACA, NEW YORK

PLATE 26

ITHACA, NEW YORK

PLATE 27

STATEN ISLAND, NEW YORK

PLATE 28

STATEN ISLAND, NEW YORK

STATEN ISLAND, NEW YORK

PLATE 29

CANDOR, NEW YORK

PLATE 30

ON FRONT STREET, OWEGO, NEW YORK

PLATE 31

COOPERSTOWN, NEW YORK

PRESTON HOUSE, COLLIERSVILLE, NEW YORK

PLATE 32

WILLSEYVILLE, TIOGA COUNTY, NEW YORK

PLATE 33

COOPERSTOWN, NEW YORK

PLATE 34

GREAT NECK, LONG ISLAND, NEW YORK

PLATE 35

RANDOLPH, NEW YORK

PLATE 36

GREAT NECK, LONG ISLAND, NEW YORK

MILLER HOUSE, LUDLOWVILLE, NEW YORK

PLATE 37

RANDOLPH, NEW YORK

MONTOUR FALLS, NEW YORK

PLATE 38

HARPERSFIELD, NEW YORK

HARPERSFIELD, NEW YORK

PLATE 39

A DOORWAY AT RANDOLPH, NEW YORK

A DOORWAY AT DERUYTER, NEW YORK

PENNSYLVANIA

PLATE 40

THE PORTICO AT ANDALUSIA, BUCKS COUNTY, PENNSYLVANIA, 1834-36

PLATE 41

LOCUST GROVE, JOHN PRICE WETHERILL HOUSE, NEAR PROFECTORY STATION, PENNSYLVANIA, 1843

PLATE 42

THE FATLANDS, AUDUBON, PENNSYLVANIA

PLATE 43

ROBERT'S HOUSE, 19th AND WALNUT STREETS, PHILADELPHIA
Now demolished

PLATE 44

REED HOUSE, 1601 CHESTNUT STREET, PHILADELPHIA
Now demolished

PLATE 45

PORTICO ROW, SOUTH SIDE OF SPRUCE STREET FROM 9th TO 10th STREETS, PHILADELPHIA

PLATE 46

1109 WALNUT STREET, PHILADELPHIA
Now demolished

PLATE 47

212 SOUTH 4th STREET, PHILADELPHIA

PLATE 48

PORTICO DOORWAY, GOWEN HOUSE, MOUNT AIRY, PHILADELPHIA

DOORWAY, 715 SPRUCE STREET, PHILADELPHIA

*NEW JERSEY*

PLATE 49

VAN WINKLE RESIDENCE, NEW MARKET, NEW JERSEY

PLATE 50

HOUSES AT METUCHEN, NEW JERSEY

PLATE 51

SEEBRING RESIDENCE, PLAINFIELD, NEW JERSEY

PLATE 52

AGNEW RESIDENCE, NEW BRUNSWICK, NEW JERSEY

PLATE 53

EWING HOUSE, MORRISTOWN, NEW JERSEY

PRINCETON, NEW JERSEY

PLATE 54

A DOORWAY AT BORDENTOWN, NEW JERSEY

DELAWARE AND MARYLAND

PLATE 55

WILMINGTON, DELAWARE

PLATE 56

107 WEST MONUMENT STREET, BALTIMORE

PLATE 57

119 WEST FRANKLIN STREET, BALTIMORE

PLATE 58

604 CATHEDRAL STREET, BALTIMORE

PLATE 59

515 PARK AVENUE, BALTIMORE

PLATE 60

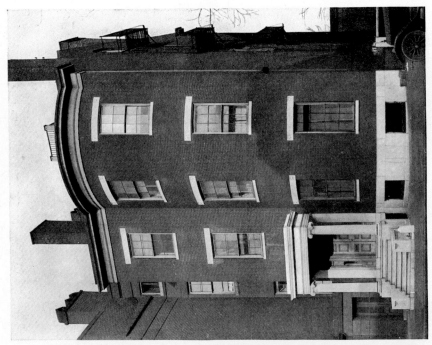

118 WEST FRANKLIN STREET, BALTIMORE

105 WEST FRANKLIN STREET, BALTIMORE

PLATE 61

8 WEST MOUNT VERNON STREET, BALTIMORE

# THE OLD NORTHWEST
*OHIO, ILLINOIS, MICHIGAN*

*OHIO*

PLATE 62

KELLEY HOUSE, COLUMBUS, OHIO

PLATE 63

NORWALK, OHIO

PLATE 64

GUTHERIE HOUSE, ZANESVILLE, OHIO

PLATE 65

WARREN, OHIO

PLATE 66

TALMADGE, OHIO

PLATE 67

PHI GAMMA DELTA HOUSE, GRANVILLE, OHIO

PLATE 68

CHAGRIN FALLS, OHIO

PLATE 69

HOUSE BETWEEN CHAGRIN FALLS AND SOLON, OHIO

PLATE 70

HOUSE NEAR WELLINGTON, OHIO

PLATE 71

HURST HOUSE, WEST OF ROCKY RIVER, OHIO

SINGLETARY HOUSE, STREETSBORO, OHIO

PLATE 72

BALDWIN BUSS HOUSE, HUDSON, SUMMIT COUNTY, OHIO

PLATE 73

HOUSE WEST OF ASHTABULA, OHIO

PLATE 74

NORWALK, OHIO

PLATE 75

KIRTLAND, OHIO

PLATE 76

PICKERING HOUSE, ST. CLAIRSVILLE, OHIO

GAYLORD HOUSE, SILVER LAKE, OHIO

PLATE 77

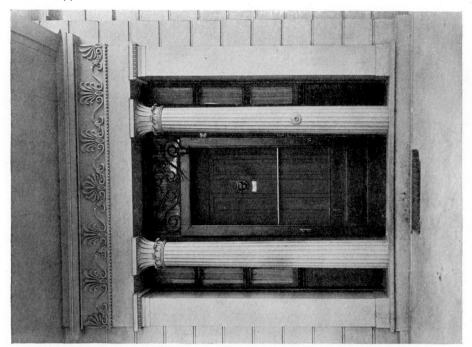

DOORWAY, PHI GAMMA DELTA HOUSE, GRANVILLE, OHIO

EAST PORCH, KELLEY HOUSE, COLUMBUS, OHIO

PLATE 78

DOORWAY, 405 FRONT STREET, MARIETTA, OHIO

DOORWAY OF BALDWIN BUSS HOUSE, HUDSON, OHIO

PLATE 79

A DOORWAY AT MADISON, LAKE COUNTY, OHIO

DOORWAY, ELWELL HOUSE, WILLOUGHBY, OHIO

PLATE 80

DOORWAY, DINING-HALL, WESTERN RESERVE COLLEGE, HUDSON, OHIO

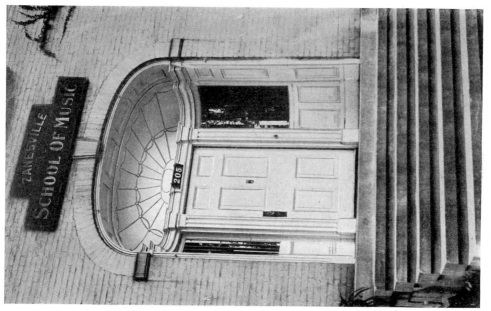

DOORWAY, BUCKINGHAM HOUSE, ZANESVILLE, OHIO

*ILLINOIS*

PLATE 81

THE McKINNEY HOUSE, PEORIA, ILLINOIS, BUILT IN 1847 BY JUDGE PETERS
Now destroyed

PLATE 82

THE MORRON HOUSE, PEORIA, ILLINOIS. BUILT IN 1848 BY JOHN REYNOLDS. ULRICHSON, ARCHITECT, CAME FROM PENNSYLVANIA

MICHIGAN

PLATE 83

THE PIKE HOUSE, FULTON STREET, GRAND RAPIDS, MICHIGAN

PLATE 84

SMITH HOUSE, GRASS LAKE, MICHIGAN, 1840

PLATE 85

ANN ARBOR, MICHIGAN

PLATE 86

MILLS HOUSE, TIPTON, MICHIGAN, 1850

PLATE 87

JAMES McALLISTER HOUSE, TECUMSEH, MICHIGAN, 1839

PLATE 88

TIPTON. MICHIGAN

PLATE 89

SMITH TAVERN, CLINTON, MICHIGAN. 1840

PLATE 90

HOUSE OF COLONEL JAMES R. SMITH, MONROE, MICHIGAN, 1858

PLATE 91

HOUSE OF DAVID CARPENTER, BLISSFIELD, MICHIGAN, 1852

PLATE 92

ANDERSON HOUSE, TECUMSEH, MICHIGAN

NEAR MANCHESTER, MICHIGAN

PLATE 93

THOMAS HOWLAND HOUSE, NEAR ADRIAN, MICHIGAN, 1840

A TYPICAL MICHIGAN FARMHOUSE, BUILT BY BUTLER TREAT IN 1851, NEAR TECUMSEH, MICHIGAN

PLATE 94

MATTHEWS HOUSE, NEAR CLINTON, MICHIGAN

PLATE 95

DOCTOR MASON HOUSE, DUNDEE, MICHIGAN

PEAVEY HOUSE, NEAR TIPTON, MICHIGAN

PLATE 96

DOORWAY ON LA PLAISANCE BAY ROAD, LENAWEE COUNTY, MICHIGAN

# THE SOUTH ATLANTIC SEABOARD
*VIRGINIA, NORTH CAROLINA, SOUTH CAROLINA, SOUTHEASTERN GEORGIA, FLORIDA*

*VIRGINIA*

PLATE 97

"ARLINGTON," ALEXANDRIA COUNTY, VIRGINIA

PLATE 98

"MANTUA," NORTHUMBERLAND COUNTY, VIRGINIA

PLATE 99

"BERRY HILL," CHARLOTTE COUNTY, VIRGINIA

PLATE 100

THE ARCHER RESIDENCE, RICHMOND, VIRGINIA

NORTH CAROLINA

PLATE 101

MARTICHAL RESIDENCE, RALEIGH, NORTH CAROLINA

PLATE 102

DOORWAY OF THE MARTICHAL RESIDENCE, RALEIGH, NORTH CAROLINA

SOUTH CAROLINA

PLATE 103

MIKELL RESIDENCE, MONTAGU AND RUTLEDGE STREETS, CHARLESTON, SOUTH CAROLINA, ABOUT 1853

PLATE 104

MIKELL RESIDENCE, CHARLESTON, SOUTH CAROLINA, ABOUT 1853

RUTLEDGE AND MONTAGU STREETS, CHARLESTON,
SOUTH CAROLINA

PLATE 105

THE MILLER RESIDENCE, CHARLESTON, SOUTH CAROLINA

PLATE 106

9 BAY STREET, CHARLESTON, SOUTH CAROLINA

PLATE 107

ALSTON RESIDENCE, CHARLESTON, SOUTH CAROLINA

PLATE 108

LADSON RESIDENCE, CHARLESTON, SOUTH CAROLINA

PLATE 109

CHARLES ALSTON HOUSE, CHARLESTON, SOUTH CAROLINA

WILLIAM MASON SMITH HOUSE, CHARLESTON, SOUTH CAROLINA

PLATE 110

CHARLESTON, SOUTH CAROLINA

PLATE III

LANES RESIDENCE, BEAUFORT, SOUTH CAROLINA

BEAUFORT, SOUTH CAROLINA

SOUTHEASTERN GEORGIA

PLATE 112

SAVANNAH, GEORGIA

PLATE 113

AN ENTRANCE AT SAVANNAH, GEORGIA

AN ENTRANCE AT SAVANNAH, GEORGIA

329 ABERCORIE STREET, SAVANNAH, GEORGIA

A CAST IRON BALCONY AT SAVANNAH, GEORGIA

PLATE 114

PLATE 115

PORTICO OF THE TELLFAIR ART GALLERY, SAVANNAH, GEORGIA

CAST IRON RAILING AT TELLFAIR MUSEUM

PLATE 116

THE HERMITAGE, SAVANNAH, GEORGIA. BUILT 1830

*FLORIDA*

PLATE 117

NOARING HOUSE, MARIANNA, FLORIDA

ELY HOUSE, MARIANNA, FLORIDA

# THE OLD SOUTHWEST
*NORTHWESTERN GEORGIA, ALABAMA, MISSISSIPPI, LOUISIANA*

NORTHWESTERN GEORGIA

PLATE 118

COLUMBUS, GEORGIA

PLATE 119

COLUMBUS, GEORGIA

PLATE 120

FANTAINE HOUSE, COLUMBUS, GEORGIA

AT COLUMBUS, GEORGIA

PLATE 121

642 PRINCE STREET, ATHENS, GEORGIA

PLATE 122

ATHENS, GEORGIA

PLATE 123

HOUSE ON PRINCE STREET, ATHENS, GEORGIA

PLATE 124

425 HILL STREET, ATHENS, GEORGIA

PLATE 125

BRADSHAW HOUSE, ATHENS, GEORGIA

PLATE 126

LA GRANGE, GEORGIA

PLATE 127

WILSON HOUSE, LA GRANGE, GEORGIA

DALLIS HOUSE, LA GRANGE, GEORGIA

PLATE 128

W. REEVES' HOUSE, LA GRANGE, GEORGIA

PLATE 129

TODD HOUSE, LA GRANGE, GEORGIA

PLATE 130

HILL HOUSE, LA GRANGE, GEORGIA

PLATE 131

NUMOSA HALL, ROSWELL, GEORGIA

PLATE 132

EXECUTIVE MANSION, MILLEDGEVILLE, GEORGIA

PLATE 133

EMORY SPEAR HOUSE, MACON, GEORGIA

PLATE 134

COLEMAN HOUSE, MACON, GEORGIA

PLATE 135

RALPH SMALL HOUSE, MACON, GEORGIA

PLATE 136

DOCTOR MILLER'S HOUSE, MACON, GEORGIA

PLATE 137

ATLANTA, GEORGIA

ALABAMA

PLATE 138

MONTGOMERY, ALABAMA

MONTGOMERY, ALABAMA

PLATE 139

D. L. ROSEMAN HOUSE, TUSCALOOSA, ALABAMA

PLATE 140

COCHRANE PLACE, TUSCALOOSA, ALABAMA
Brick columns, Cast-iron capitals, Silver hardware

PLATE 141

**BATTLE HOUSE, TUSCALOOSA, ALABAMA**
Stucco, lined and coloured (not painted) to imitate pink and yellow marble in its original condition

PLATE 142

SPENCE HOUSE, TUSCALOOSA, ALABAMA

PLATE 143

PRESIDENT'S HOUSE, UNIVERSITY OF ALABAMA, TUSCALOOSA, ALABAMA

Nichols, Architect—an Englishman

PLATE 144

HUNTSVILLE, ALABAMA

PLATE 145

HUNTSVILLE, ALABAMA

PLATE 146

HUNTSVILLE, ALABAMA

PLATE 147

CASEY HOMESTEAD, NEAR AUBURN, ALABAMA

RUSH HOMESTEAD, NEAR TUSKEGEE, ALABAMA

PLATE 148

COBB HOUSE, TUSKEGEE, ALABAMA

TUSKEGEE, ALABAMA

PLATE 149

A COTTAGE AT TUSKEGEE, ALABAMA

AT TUSKEGEE, ALABAMA

PLATE 150

A "RAISED" COTTAGE AT AUBURN, ALABAMA

A COTTAGE AT AUBURN, ALABAMA

PLATE 151

HUNTSVILLE, ALABAMA

*MISSISSIPPI*

PLATE 152

"MONMOUTH," HOME OF MRS. A. G. GARVIN, NATCHEZ, MISSISSIPPI

PLATE 153

"STANTON HALL," RESIDENCE OF R. T. CLARK, NATCHEZ, MISSISSIPPI

PLATE 154

"DUNLEITH," HOME OF J. N. CARPENTER, NATCHEZ, MISSISSIPPI

PLATE 155

A PLANTATION HOME AT NATCHEZ, MISSISSIPPI

REAR OF SARGENT HOUSE, NEAR NATCHEZ, MISSISSIPPI

PLATE 156

AUBURN HOUSE, NATCHEZ, MISSISSIPPI

A PLANTATION HOME AT NATCHEZ, MISSISSIPPI

PLATE 157

"ROSALIE," HOME OF MRS. E. S. RUMBLE, NATCHEZ, MISSISSIPPI

"DEVEREAUX," HOME OF MRS. BAYARD SHIELDS, NATCHEZ, MISSISSIPPI

PLATE 158

NATCHEZ, MISSISSIPPI

GENERAL GRANT'S HEADQUARTERS, VICKSBURG, MISSISSIPPI

PLATE 159

NATCHEZ, MISSISSIPPI

LOUISIANA

PLATE 160

232 RAMPART STREET, NEW ORLEANS

2221 PRYTANIA STREET, NEW ORLEANS

PLATE 161

BAKER HOMESTEAD, NEAR THIBODAUX, ON BAYOU LA FOURCHE, LOUISIANA
Flanking wings on both sides.   Order executed in stucco

A PLANTATION HOME ON BAYOU LA FOURCHE, NEAR THIBODAUX, LOUISIANA

PLATE 162

"HERMITAGE," THE FIRST HOME OF THE BRINGIER FAMILY, ASCENSION PARISH, LOUISIANA
All interior trim and stair in solid walnut from trees on the plantation

"THREE OAKS," A PLANTATION HOME NEAR CHALMETTE, LOUISIANA

PLATE 163

**PLANTATION HOUSE NEAR CONVENT, LOUISIANA**
Unique grouping of columns

**ACROSS RIVER FROM NEW ORLEANS, LOUISIANA**

PLATE 164

BAYOU ST. JOHN, LOUISIANA

PLATE 165

STOVER HOUSE, NEW ORLEANS
A fine example of "Raised Cottage" type

IN THE OLD AMERICAN SECTION, NEW ORLEANS

PLATE 166

IN "GARDEN DISTRICT," NEW ORLEANS

IN "GARDEN DISTRICT," NEW ORLEANS

PLATE 167

BEAUREGARD HOMESTEAD, "VIEUX CARRÉE" DISTRICT, NEW ORLEANS

IN "GARDEN DISTRICT," NEW ORLEANS

PLATE 168

AT JACKSON AND CHESTNUT STREETS, NEW ORLEANS

# INDEX

# INDEX

Adam, Brothers, 30, 31
Alabama, 5, 8, 46
　University of, 91
Alleghanies, 6, 59, 83, 86, 95
American Revolution, 28, 44, 83
Amphiprostyle, Octastyle, 18
Andalusia, near Philadelphia, 47, 66
Antae, 64, 66, 70
Arcade, see Basement Story, 41
Arches, 64
Architects in the Republic, 13, 17, 34, 36,
　37, 38, 39, 41, 42, 44, 47, 91
　Amateur, 13, 34, 36, 37, 38, 41, 42, 44, 91
　European, 17, 20, 24, 29, 30, 33, 42, 47
　In the colonies, 13, 34
Architecture, America's independent, vii,
　3, 11, 12, 14, 27, 33, 42, 44, 85, 89
Architraves, 66, 75, 90
　Door, 50, 64, 73
　Window, 50, 64, 73
Arlington, Alexandria County, Va., 36, 46
Ashlar, see Stone, 53
Athens, Ga., Cast iron balcony, 76
Atlantic Seaboard, vii, 5, 6
Attic, 64

Balconies, 76, 90
Balusters, 75
Basement Story, 41, 91
Bays, 55
Benjamin, Asher, 38
　"The Architect or Practical House Car-
　　penter," 1830, 41, 48, 50, 68, 70, 72
Berry Hill, Va., 48
Biddle, Nicholas, 46, 47
Books on Architecture, Influence of, x, xi,
　18, 24, 28, 29, 31, 32, 33, 34, 41. See also
　Handbooks on Architecture
Boston, 37, 38
Brady, J. C., 39
Brick, 53, 64, 79, 88
"Brickbuilder, The," 1904, 88
Bryant, William Cullen, 44
Bullfinch, Charles, 37, 38
Burr, Thaddeus, House, Fairfield, Conn.,
　34, 35, 39

Campbell, Colin, "Vitruvius Britannicus,"
　23, 24
　" Palladio," 28
Canada, 83
Capitals, 53
　Corinthian, 53, 88
　Doric, 41
　Ionic, 91
Carolinas, 5, 85, 86
"Carpenters Classic," 8
Carstairs, Thomas, 38
Carter, Elias, 39
Cast iron, Ornamental, 53, 64, 75, 76, 77, 88
Ceilings, 72
Cella, 29, 31, 41, 62
Centre blocks, 66, 75
　pieces, 72
Charleston, S. C., 90
Chimney piece, 72, 73
Cincinnati, 85
Clapboards, 53
Claridon, Ohio, Doorway of house at, 94
Clerisseau, "Monuments de Nìmes," 20
Climate, Suitability to, 11, 33, 89, 90
Cochrane, Dr. William, 88
"Cochrane Place," 1840, 88
Cockerell, S. P., 31, 36
Collaborators, vii, viii, ix
Colonade, 14, 18, 47, 59, 60, 62, 88, 90, 96
Colonial Architecture, 6, 7, 11, 12, 13, 18, 50
　53, 60, 62, 70, 73, 87, 88, 93, 94, 96
　Design; Similarity between English 18th
　　Century architecture and, 11, 12, 13
Colossal, 14, 59, 88, 90, 91, 96
Columbus, Ohio, 95
Columns, 18, 20, 46, 48, 53, 55, 59, 60, 64,
　66, 68, 70, 72, 78, 79, 88, 90
　Engaged, 66, 73
　Proportion of, 68, 70, 90
Connecticut, 85
Consoles, 64, 66
Cooper, James Fenimore, 44
Corner blocks, 66, 68, 75
　boards, 53
Cornices, 50, 90
Cotton belt, 5, 86, 87

# INDEX

Cox House, Dresden, Ohio, 68, 69
Cumberland, Md., 95
Cupola, 72, 73

Dado, 72
Davis, A. J., 39, 74
Demopolis, Ala., 91
de Tesse, Countess, 20
Doors, 50, 64
Doorway, 55, 64, 65, 66, 72, 90, 94
Downing, Andrew J., 78, 79
Dublin Society, 34

Eaves, 63
Eighteenth Century, 12, 21, 28, 30, 34, 37, 38, 72, 75, 77, 83 90
Empire styles, 43, 44
England, 12, 13, 17, 24, 28, 30, 31, 33, 36, 37, 44, 83
English Architecture, 12, 13, 27, 28
English influence, 13, 27, 28, 33, 34, 43, 44, 50
Entablature, 62, 63, 66, 70, 72, 90
Erie Canal, 96
Europe, Travels in, 13, 20, 36, 37, 47
European influence, 14, 20, 27

Fan-light, 68
Federal Architecture, 4
Finials, 75
Fire places, see Chimney pieces, 72
Florida, 11, 45, 89
Fluting, 66, 73
Fourteenth Century, 75
Frame, 53
France, 20, 36, 37, 43
French Architecture, 44
French emigrés, 43, 91
French influence, 43, 44, 86, 91
French Revolution, 43, 91
Frieze, 64
Fulton, Robert, 78

Gable, 62
Gainswood, Demopolis, Ala., 91, 92
Garden Temples, 23, 29, 31
Gates, 77
Georgia, 8, 11, 45
Georgian Architecture, 3, 12, 13

"Georgian Period, The," 1901, 12, 60, 87
Girard College, Phila., 70, 71
Governor's House at Williamsburg, 18, 19, 20, 21
Graeco-Roman school, 29, 30, 31
Great Lakes, vii, 7, 83, 86
Greece, 4, 17, 28, 46, 47, 78
Greek forms, 4, 17, 27, 29, 30, 31, 32, 33, 34, 35, 39, 41, 43, 46, 48, 50, 59, 70, 77, 78, 79, 89, 95, 96
Greek mania, 44, 45, 46, 79, 89
Greenfield, Mass., 38
Grilles, Window, 53, 64
Gulf States, vii, 11, 83, 86

Hagley, Garden temple at, for Lord Lyttelton, 29, 31
Hall, Louis, House, Osborne, Mich., 62
Hallet, Stephen, 34, 36
Halls, 88
Handbooks on Architecture, 13, 38, 48, 93, 94. See also books on Architecture
Hardware, 88
Harvey, George, 39
Hatfield, George, 36, 46
Hexastyle, 21
Hoban, James, 34
Hopper, Edward, 28

Illinois, 46
Indian, 83
    disturbances, 84
Indiana, 46, 85
Indianapolis, 95
Interiors, 72, 73, 74
Irving, Washington, 44
Italy, 37

Jamb, 68, 75
Jefferson, Thomas, 17, 18, 19, 20, 21, 22, 24, 27, 37, 39, 41, 42
Jones, Inigio, 17, 28

Kentucky, 46, 85, 86
Keystone, 66, 75
Kimball, Fiske, "Domestic Architecture of the American Colonies," N. Y., 1922, 12, 13, 14, 21
Kitchens, 88

# INDEX

Lafever, Minard, "The Modern Builder's Guide," 1833, 39, 48, 49, 50, 54, 55, 60, 61
Lake Erie, 85
Latrobe, Benjamin, 31, 36, 39, 40
L'Enfant, Major Pierre Charles, 37
Leoni, Giacoma, "Palladio," 28
Library Company of Philadelphia, 34
Lintels, 64, 68
Literature, Independent American, 44
Log cabins, 83, 84, 85
Logan Elm, Log Cabin at, 83
London, 37
Lord Lyttelton, 29
Louisiana, 46, 86

Mackay House, Willseyville, N. Y., 64, 66
Madeleine, Paris, 24, 39
Maine, 11, 45
Maine State House, 38
Maison Carreé, 20, 21
Major, Thomas, "Ruins of Paestum," 34
Marble, 53, 73
Marietta, Ohio, 85
Maryland, 86
Mc Comb, John, 38
Mc Intyre, Samuel, 38
Mezzanine, 91
Michigan, 8, 45
Mills, Robert, 36
Mississippi, vii, 5, 46, 83
Mississippi River, vii, 5, 7, 86
Missouri, 46
Mitchell, Robert, "Plans and Views in Perspective, with Description of Buildings," 31, 32, 33, 41, 43
Montgomery, Ala., House at, 59
Monticello, 18
Morse, Samuel F. B., 78
Mouldings, 41, 64, 70
Mullions, 64

Napoleon, Court of, 91
National Capitol Building, Washington. D. C., 37, 38
National Monument at Edinburgh, 39
National Road, 95
New Bedford Court House, 78

New England, 5, 38, 39, 85, 86, 87, 94
New Jersey, 45
New York, 5, 38, 39, 43, 45
New York City Hall, 38
Nichols, Mr., 91
Nicholson, 50
Nîmes, 20
Nineteenth Century, Artistic expressions in, 3, 12, 14, 53, 59, 60, 75, 77
Nomenclature, 4, 8, 27, 45, 46
No. 15 St. James Square, 29, 30
No. 1107 Walnut Street, Phila., 64, 65
No. 1109 Walnut Street, Phila., 63
North Atlantic Seaboard, 6, 45, 53, 72, 94, 95, 96
North Carolina, 45
Northern Indiana Historical Society, The, 7
Northwest, The Old, 5, 6, 7, 45, 66, 83, 85, 86, 87, 88, 91, 93, 95, 96

Ohio, 8, 45, 85
Ohio River, 5, 7, 83, 85, 87, 95
Orders, 14, 27, 33, 34, 35, 39, 41, 48, 70, 89, 90, 91, 95
  Corinthian, 70
  Doric, 70
  Ionic, 70
  Lysicrates type, 70, 71
Outbuildings, 88
Over-mantel, 73

Paestum, Temple at, 34, 46
Palladian School, 28, 30, 31
Palladio, "Four Books of Architecture," 18, 19, 20, 28
Panelling, 72
Parris, Alexander, 38
Parthenon, 39, 48
Paulding, James Kirke, 44
Pavilions, 60
Pediment, 18, 19, 20, 59, 60, 62, 63, 66, 88
Pennsylvania, 5, 45, 85
Pennsylvania, Bank of, 36
Pennsylvania State Capitol, Harrisburg, 36
Peristyle, 32, 47
Philadelphia, 36, 38, 47, 91
Pilasters, 53, 72, 73, 90

# INDEX

Plan, 19, 20 23, 43, 50, 53, 54, 55, 60, 61, 88, 91, 93

Plantation Home, 59, 60, 86, 87, 88, 96, 5, 6, 11

Porches, 90, 91

Porte Cochère, 55

Portico, 19, 20, 21, 46, 55, 60, 62, 63, 66, 88

Portsmouth, N. H., Doorway at, 66, 67

Potomac, 6, 46

Prostile Hexastile Eustile, 24

Prostyle, 47

Provence, 20

Railings, 53, 75

Ramsey, S. C., "Small Houses of the Georgian Period," London, 1919, 12, 13

Reeding, 66, 68, 73

Richmond, Va., 21

Ricketson, Daniel, 78

Roman forms, 17, 18, 20, 21, 24, 27, 28, 32, 33, 34, 41, 48, 70, 89, 96

Rome, 4, 17, 18, 20, 24, 28, 36, 78

Root, 18, 19, 20, 59, 60, 62, 96

Rotch, Joseph, House, 78

Salem, Mass., 38

Sash, 63
  bar, 64

Scientific development, 78

Seymour's, Professor, House, Hudson, Ohio, 66, 67

Shingles, 53, 84

Sidelights, 64

Siding, 53

Singletary House, Streetsboro, Ohio, 93, 94

Slaves, 5, 6, 86, 87

South Atlantic Seaboard, 6, 45, 86, 96

South Carolina, 34, 45

South Carolina State House, 34

Southwest, The Old, 6, 7, 14, 46, 59, 72, 83, 85, 86, 87, 88, 89, 91, 96

Spanish Architecture, 89

Stars, Band of, 68

Stevens, John C., House, interior of, 74

St. John's Church, New York City, 38

Stone, 53, 64, 68

Stories, Height of, 72, 90, 96

St. Paul's, London, 77

Strickland, William, 36, 40

Stuart, James, 29, 30, 31

Stuart and Revett, "Classical Antiquities of Athens," 28, 29, 34, 50

Stucco, 53

Subdivisions of the Style, 5, 6, 7, 11, 83, 85, 86, 91, 93, 96

Sussex, England, 75

Temple form, 4, 14, 17, 18, 19, 20, 21, 24, 27, 31, 32, 33, 41, 43, 46, 47, 53, 55, 59, 62, 78, 89, 95, 96

Tennessee, 86

Thompson, M. E., 39

Thornton, Dr. William, 37, 38

Towne, Ithiel, 39

Trading posts, 85

Transom, 64, 68
  circular, 64
  elliptical, 64, 68
  square, 64

Transportation, 95

Treat House, Aurora, Ohio, 68

Trellises, 53

Trims, see Architraves

Trollope, Mrs. Frances, 43

Tusculoosa, Ala., State Capitol, 91

Tuskegee, Ala., House at, 88, 89

Tuthil, Mrs. L. A., 79

Unionville, Ohio, Doorway at, 66, 69

United States, Bank of, 39, 40

Van Ness Mansion, Washington, D. C., 54, 55

Van Vorst Mansion, Jersey City, N. J., 60

Verandas, 11

Vermont, 45

Vesper Cliff, Oswego, N. Y., 72, 73

Virginia, 5, 18, 20, 45, 86

Virginia State Capitol, 20, 22, 24, 39

Virginia, University of, Pavilion, vii, 41, 42

Virginias, 85, 86

Vosoirs, 68

Walhalla, at Regensburg, 39

Wall surfaces, 72, 90

# INDEX

Walter, Thomas, 38, **71**
War of 1812, 43, 44, 84, 95
   of Greek independence, **44,** 48
Ware, Isaac, "Palladio," **28**
   " Body of Architecture," 1756, **75**
Washington, D. C., 37, 46
West Indies, 37
Westward, Migration, 5, 84, 85, 86, 93, 95
Wheeling, 95
White House, Washington, 34
Whitfield, General G. B., 91, 92

Windows, 50, 63, 64, **72**
   casement, 63
   circular headed, 63
   frieze, 63
   triple, 63
   triple sliding windows, 63
Wings, 55, 60, 62, 63, 91, 96
Wisconsin, 46
Wood, see Frame, 78, **79**
Wrought Iron, **75, 77**